INTERBOROU

FLEET

by

Joe Cunningham

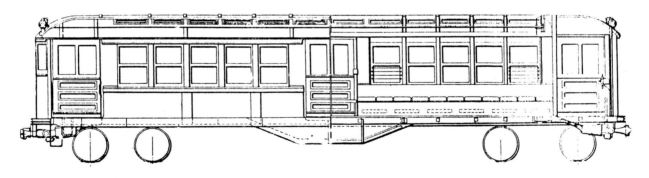

"To Isabel Cunningham for she introduced me to the subway then endured and encouraged my explorations with the patience of a saint."

Library of Congress 96-061449

ISBN 0-9645765-3-8

Tile, Chandeliers, Stained glass skylights and uniformed platform conductors
are ready to begin a new era in New York Cities history -the subway.

City Hall
Subway Station
New York

2

PHASE I:
THE PIONEER EFFORT

by Joe Cunningham

THE SEARCH FOR AN OPTIMAL VEHICLE

Every aspect of the construction and equipment of New York's first subway represented an unprecedented challenge to the best minds in a variety of engineering disciplines. Although the tunnel and right of way were to be owned by the City of New York, the operating components were the responsibility of the operator. Furthermore, there were no subway predecessors from which concepts could be derived. At that time, the elevated network of the Manhattan Railway Company was the world's most extensive rapid transit operation. Then pursuing an eighteen million dollar electrification project, the experience and practice of the elevated Company supplied substantial data for component engineering on the Interborough.

Express trains on the subway were scheduled to average 40 MPH, a velocity found at that time only on passenger trains of mainline railroads. Both the management and engineers of the Rapid Transit Subway Construction Company approached each task in a logical and forthright manner. The needs were defined, the best engineering talent retained, and the optimal method determined. At that point the most experienced manufacturer was contracted to supply the components.

The project had to be completed successfully and on time. Failure was not an option. Nor were delays, cost overruns or other boon-doggles. As the project took place in the capital of the world's press, it was monitored rigorously in every detail. The firms involved would have been ruined by failure. The only option was success, an out come which would guarantee future opportunity.

The pioneer nature of the subway resulted in the use of techniques which guaranteed reliability and practicality in both operation and maintenance. Although the project was undertaken by John B. McDonald's Rapid Transit Subway Construction Company, financing was provided by August Belmont Jr., heir to his father's banking fortune and also the American agent of the European Rothschild banking syndicate. William Barclay Parsons was the chief engineer of the City's Board of Rapid Transit Railroad Commissioners. In that capacity, he was obligated to oversee every aspect of the engineering and construction of the new line. As it happened, both Belmont and Parsons maintained a direct interest in the engineering, design and construction of the necessary operating hardware.

The size of the car was determined at the outset, the dimensions being limited by the clearances of the tunnel under construction. Station platforms were to align with the floor of the car, thus eliminating the need for steps. The program was initiated with an extensive survey of every passenger transit vehicle design then operating in the United States. Some foreign vehicles were examined as well. It was determined that the interior configuration of the Manhattan elevated cars maximized seating while facilitating the movement of passengers. Four pairs of transverse seats were located at the center of the car while longitudinal seats were located under the windows on both sides of each end. The program was placed under the direction of George Gibbs, one of the most influential railroad experts in U.S. history.

AUGUST BELMONT

The first New York subway car, the August Belmont, resembled the elegant private street railway vehicles of the period. The interior explored the possibility of First Class service, an amenity which never materialized. *[AL/EBW]*

John B. McDonald

(Top left)
The tradional lines of the railway coach are evident in this view at the Wason plant in Springfield Mass.
[AL/EBW]

[Opposite page]
Experimental Composite car #2 John B McDonald poses with Interbrough officials at the 99th St. Shops of the Manhattan Elevated Railway. *[NG]*

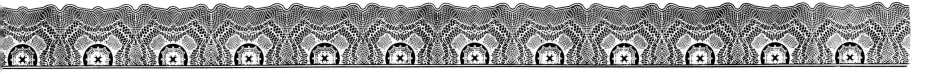

Enter Mr. Gibbs

George Gibbs enjoyed phenomenal success in a career that spanned more than a half century. Having earned his engineering degree at the prestigious Stevens Institute of Hoboken, N.J., Gibbs had more than a decade of railway mechanical engineering experience before making the move which determined his future. In 1895, he was appointed to the electric locomotive development program at Westinghouse Electric & Manufacturing Co., a joint effort with the Baldwin Locomotive Company. He soon became a luminary in that field.

Gibbs possessed the rare ability to manage simultaneously a number of projects, any one of which would have occupied fully the talents of other men. At the time he was retained for the subway car project, Gibbs was also a member of the commission to electrify Grand Central, the consultant on electric traction for New York's new Pennsylvania station, and the director of the electrification program of the Long Island Rail Road. Subsequent to his involvement with the subway project, Gibbs was named first vice-president of Westinghouse, Church, Kerr & Company, the engineering affiliate of Westinghouse Electric.

He then joined his assistant Earnest Rowland Hill to form Gibbs & Hill, an engineering giant with worldwide credentials. In succeeding decades, the firm became a leader in the design and construction of alternating current railroad electrification. Gibbs continued his involvement with railroad assignments until the late 1930s, the leading figure in the long distance electrification of the Pennsylvania Railroad. Not only was that program the nation's most extensive, much of it is still intact as Amtrak's Northeast Corridor.

On accepting the subway car assignment, Gibbs recommended steel construction. That proposal met with a chorus of objections from the established car builders. It was said that the time for research and development would be lengthy, expensive and uncertain. Gibbs was forced to acquiesce, but it was the last time he would do so.

THE COMPOSITE COMPROMISE

Faced with utter indifference and even contempt from the established car builders, Gibbs developed a compromise while he continued to press the steel car concept. His "Composite" car of wood with steel framing was the most rigorously engineered rail car in history. Four feet longer than the standard Manhattan elevated car, it incorporated a variety of modifications. The upper sashes of the windows opened instead of the lowers, a safety measure given the tight curves and limited clearances within the tunnels. Likewise, the open boarding platforms of elevated cars were replaced by enclosed vestibules of the type that were gaining acceptance on most railroads.

In an effort to maximize interior space, the sidewalls of the car included a "batter" or out wardslope from the roof line to the window sill. Such a configuration provided greater "elbow room" at the seat level without compromising the clearance "envelope" at the roof. Fire hazards were a major consideration. To that end, the walls of the car below the windo wsill level were sheathed with copper in an effort to provide protection from external flames. Developed by William Appleyard of the New York, New Haven & Hartford railroad, the sheathing was used by several roads to eliminate the frequent painting required by exposed wood. Sheathing as a flame retardant was unique to the New York subway.

Journalists of the day were impressed, referring to the "flaming, burnished sides" of the cars. Unlike the painted lettering of most rail vehicles, the copper sides facilitated the use of "acid-etched" characters. After the introduction of steel cars, the subway crews termed the Composite cars "Coppersides." The name persisted after the copper was removed when the fleet was transferred to service on the Manhattan elevated lines. Although it has been suggested that the removal of the sheathing was due to World War I, it is likely that the change was occasioned by more mundane concerns. Weight was an issue where elevated structures were concerned and World War I did not generate the intensive scrap drives that developed during World War II. Thus it is more likely that the copper was removed to reduce weight. No doubt the salvage value of so much copper plate was also attractive to a company in the midst of an expansion program!

Two sample cars were assembled by the Wason Company in 1902. Named the August Belmont and the John B. McDonald, each was fitted with different appliances to determine the components best suited to subway service. Different styles of seats were installed as a premium "first class" service was being given some consideration. Ornate lighting fixtures, different ceilings, and several roof ventilation schemes were among the concepts explored. The most significant experiment was a sliding vestibule door which retracted into a "pocket" in the side of the car body. A patented invention of

George Gibbs, the concept became an axiom of transit car design. The competing designs included a cumbersome folding door developed by the Pullman Company which obstructed a portion of the boarding vestibule even when folded.

THE COMPOSITE FLEET

With the basic car configuration determined, five hundred Composite cars were ordered from four builders; the Wason, Stephenson, St. Louis, and Jewett companies. Unlike the steel car proposal, the orders were accepted readily despite a substantial backlog of orders. All were standardized, the frivolous concept of first class service having been dropped.

Passenger safety remained a pressing concern. Heavy "collision posts" were included, those consisting of wooden beams so located as to absorb the impact of end to end collisions. Electrical safety was addressed by L.B. Stilwell, a railway and electrical expert whose credentials included the Niagara Falls hydroelectric project. His previous effort on the Manhattan elevated railway's electrification program met with spectacular success. At that time, most electric railways experienced frequent fires on small fleets of several dozen cars. By comparison, there were no electrical fires on the Manhattan Company's fleet of more than one thousand cars during theeighteen months that the system had been in operation.

Stilwell's program included rigorous safety inspections and periodic subjection of electrical components to high voltage tests. Asbestos "Transite" panels protected the car floors from the electrical components mounted beneath the car. "Electrobestos" insulation was placed around the electrical switchboard at the end of the car. All wiring was confined to metallic ducts and the components beneath the car were arranged to minimize the length and complexity of cabling.

The ducts were of the "Loricated" type which had been developed for large buildings. Coated with porcelain to prevent chafing of wire insulation, the ducts also facilitated the installation of cables without damage. "Bell-Mouth" connectors, developed for marine wiring, were used at all junctions. Rubber blocks in the flared ends held the wires in place and prevented abrasion of the insulation. All wiring which was subjected to flexing due to motion was insulated with multiple layers of "Para-rubber" with metallic braid providing protection against abrasion. In short, no effort or expense was spared to prevent electrical fires.

The carbody was similar to railroad coaches of the period. Exposed wood was finished in Tuscan Red with Burnt Orange trim, the interior was paneled wood with glossy white ceilings. Electric light and heat were included, ventilation was provided by clerestory roof vents arranged such that the motion of the car provided air exchange. The seats were canvas backed rattan on wooden frames. "Pantasote" roller shades with adjustable catches were located at all side windows. A pair of sliding doors gave access to the end vestibules which were open to the elements at the outer end.

A single sliding door at each side of the vestibule provided access to the station platform. Controlled by levers from cranks on the end of the car, the doors were operated by a "guard" (trainman) stationed between every pair of adjoining vestibules. Similar to the "gatemen" who operated the gates on the end platforms of elevated cars, the arrangement was acceptable in an era of minimal wages, no benefits, and a large pool of available, unskilled labor.

Operating plans called for approximately 65% of the cars in each train to be equipped with motors. On such cars, operating controls were located at the right side of both vestibules. The controls were simple, a "master" controller for the motors, an air brake valve and guages, whistle and several electrical switches. A swinging door protected the equipment at all points except at the ends of the train.

At those positions, the door was secured across the opening at the outer end of the vestibule to prevent the entry of wind and weather. It may well have been the first instance that a railroad car vestibule was closed at the outer end. When so configured, the vestibule was closed to passengers by the locking of the pair of sliding doors which accessed the interior of the car, the entire vestibule space available only to the motorman.

Three hundred forty cars were equipped with motors. Such cars carried a pair of four color marker lamps on the roof at both ends of the car. Capable of displaying a total of sixteen different color combinations, the marker lamps indicated route and service options to subway personnel. Brackets permitted the placement of kerosene lamps beneath each of the end windows of the car. Displaying white at the front, red at the rear, the use of kerosene was intended to assure visibilityin the event of an electric failure on the car.

The propulsion system was simple. One truck carried a pair of 200 hp motors, one geared to each axle, an assembly which was the most powerful available at that time. A product of the Baldwin Locomotive Works, it was designed for durability and ease of maintenance. The motors were supplied by both General Electric and Westinghouse. The control system was the standard G.E. Type M which utilized the Sprague multiple unit patents. The Sprague system employed control switches on each car to effect the control of the motors on that car. A "trainline" circuit extending the length of the train connected the control switches on each car with the motorman's controller at the head of the train. The entire assembly was basic, operated by line voltage drawn directly from the third rail.

The train was accelerated manually by advancing the master controller through a range of twelve steps. A novel feature permitted the handle of the master controller to be moved to the limit while a current relay retarded the advancement of the electrical contacts until the motor current had declined to a level at which the control could be advanced safely. Though designed for a nominal supply voltage of 625 V.D.C., the propulsion system was engineered to operate on voltages as low as 575 without any degradation of performance.

Other innovations included a "Dead Man's" button on the controller which had to be held to sustain operation. If released due to fatigue or injury, power was removed and an "emergency" brake application ensued automatically. Third rail power collection was provided by hinged "slipper" shoes which projected outward to ride the surface of a new "Safety" third rail. Unlike the exposed third rail which was common to most transit lines, the Safety design included a protection board suspended above the power conducting rail.

Heavy line voltage "bus" jumper cables connected the third rail shoe circuits of all motor cars and also provided light and heat in the unpowered "trailer" cars (which were not equipped with third rail shoes.) While the jumper assured reliable operation of the entire train, it posed a significant problem at the "section breaks" or gaps between third rail zones. In the event a train crossed the gap into a zone which was deenergized, the jumper circuit would energize that section with potentially disastrous results. To prevent such mishaps, it was necessary to install special "section break" signals in advance of all third rail gaps.

An automatic air brake similar to that employed on railroad passenger trains and elevated cars was installed. Motor driven pumps supplied the air. The term "automatic" indicated that a loss of pressure would produce a full "emergency" application of the brakes. Emergency brake valves were installed on the leading edge of the trucks of all motor cars. Such valves could be engaged by the arms of the "automatic train stops" located at all mainline signals. The arm was raised whenever the signal displayed a stop aspect,

thus foiling any effort to pass. The arm lowered only when the signal cleared or a special key was inserted in a receptacle near the signal. The latter feature permitted special train movements and also the passage of trains in the event of defects in the signal system.

As the contractor held the right to lease the subway for operation, the development of alloperating hardware was transferred to the new Interborough Rapid Transit Company in 1902. As operating lessee, the Interborough company assumed all responsibility for the purchase, installation and maintenance of the operating components. The cars were delivered as unfinished coaches, the components installed initially at the 129th Street shops of the Manhattan elevated system. Later deliveries were routed to the new Interborough shop at 147th Street. With the operating hardware in place, the new cars were tested without passengers on the Second Avenue elevated line.

The use of the 129th Street shop and the Second Avenue line was simplified by the Interborough's lease of the Manhattan Railway Company in April, 1903. Although the Manhattan elevated company equipment and crews remained separate, engineering personnel was exchanged as needed and joint public services were operated.

Delivered from early 1903 through mid-1904, the new subway cars were hailed by the builders and also by the railway trade press. Gibbs was not so sanguine. Though satisfied with the product, he believed the cars obsolete vehicles which would never have been constructed were it not for the intransigence of the car builders. A man searching always for the new and improved, he intended to force the development of steel cars. With support from the Interborough management, he sought a means by which the established car builders might be bypassed. His quest was rewarded with the assistance of an outside agent.

THE STEEL REVOLUTION

An External Ally

The whims of the car builders notwithstanding, a number of railroad executives favored the development of steel cars. One was in a position to force the issue. Alexander Johnston Cassatt, one of the most dynamic and innovative executives in the history of U.S. railroads agreed. As head of the Pennsylvania Railroad, the nation's foremost transportation giant, he had spearheaded innovation in many aspects of railroad technology. Cassatt's administration had embarked on a one hundred million dollar venture: the penetration of the rivers on both sides of Manhattan Island and the construction of a magnificent new station. A civil engineer by training, Cassatt made no secret of his disdain for the operation of wooden cars through the long subaqueous tunnels. Any research effort on steel cars was of interest and potential benefit to his company.

Alexander Cassatt and his son Robert 1894-1895, as painted by his sister Mary Cassatt. *Philadelphia Museum of Art*

Gibbs enjoyed direct access to the railroad executive as a result of his role in the electrification of both Penn Station and that of the Long Island Rail Road, a recent acquisition of the Pennsylvania. Thus it happened that an experimental steel subway car was constructed at the Pennsylvania's Altoona (Pa) Shop which boasted the best facilities and most skilled manpower to be found. In addition to the usual maintenance tasks, the facility produced substantial numbers of new locomotives and cars annually.

The Test Car

Construction began in the latter half of 1903, and the world's first steel passenger car was delivered to the Interborough in December. Although it failed stringent weight limitations, the car succeeded magnificently in other respects. It not only proved the practicality of steel construction, it proved many of Gibbs' claims. The inherent strength of the riveted steel body was such that the walls could be thinner, permitting larger vestibules and also eliminating the side batter of the Composite car.

The strict weight limitations stemmed from the fact that the Composite cars employed the most powerful traction hardware available. Any substantial increase in the weight of a steel car would have degraded performance and jeopardized planned schedules. While the car was of great interest, that weight problem would have to be resolved before a steel subway car would be practical.

Ironically, the wisdom of Gibbs and the Interborough management was then demonstrated by a fire in the new Paris Metro. Scores died and many others were injured or crippled. Clearly, steel car construction was desirable, the problem was weight reduction. Though busy with a multitude of projects, Gibbs had followed the experimental program and derived a practical solution.

Although the Interborough board members were willing to acquire Gibbs' revised and unproven design in bulk, the car builders remained as intransigent as ever. A torrent of criticism was showered on the program. Absurd claims of potential hazards were made and the Composite was declared the best possible vehicle. Gibbs counterattacked with rapier-like precision, demolishing his critics.

His critics alleged that a steel car would become twisted in the event of an accident, thus trapping injured passengers; others claimed that it would present an electrocution hazard in the event of a derailment. It was declared that the car would be intolerably noisy, suffer temperature extremes, even shake apart from harmonic vibrations!

Gibbs responded to the serious concern for safety by noting that wooden cars were known to crush completely in the event of an accident while steel framing showed less tendency to deform on impact. He noted that any flame resistance provided by the copper sheathing of the Composite design would be compromised if not destroyed entirely by the splintering of the wooden sides during a collision.

As for the electrocution hazard, Gibbs noted acerbically that a steel car body would short circuit any electrical conductor with which it came into contact, thus triggering circuit breaker action that would remove power. A wooden car would be unlikely to cause power to be removed, allowing the energized power rail to present a hazard to survivors of the collision!

As for the more frivolous allegations, he remarked that proper construction and maintenance techniques would obviate any noise problem, while insulation would address temperature concerns. As for the cars shaking to pieces? There were a plethora of steel industrial and transportation structures around the city which had withstood intensive vibrations for decades without such catastrophic failures!

The "Gibbs" Fleet

As is so often the case, progress was made by a secondary supplier eager to break into the ranks of the leaders. In the case of the steel car, it was the American Car & Foundry Company. The company contracted with the Interborough to supply two hundred steel cars of Gibbs' revised design. A subsequent contract raised the total to three hundred and construction began in the late Spring of 1904. The innovation which made the new design practical was the elimination of a heavy underframe in favor of steel side girders which supported the load in the same manner as do the sides of "gondola" type railroad freight cars. Thus it was possible to employ a structural frame which was so light that additional support was needed at the center during assembly to prevent destructive deformation from its own weight. With the side girders in place, the frame became a steel box so rigid that a full test load produced a frame deflection of only 1/32", a strength never achieved previously.

Similar to the Composite car in other respects, the new steel car contained some wood, primarily in the roof. Constructed of wood pulp board, the exterior was covered with canvas "duck" cloth. The interior ceiling headliner was "scratch brushed" aluminum that reflected light to produce a brighter interior. Aluminum was a new "wonder" metal made economical by new refining technology. It was employed for a number of interior fittings, with a consequent reduction in weight when substituted for steel. Additional aluminum was incorporated into the cars constructed under the second contract. The cars were finished in Tuscan Red with Burnt Orange window frames, gold leaf lettering and pinstriping.

Though brighter, the interior appeared stark in comparison with that of the Composite. With flat walls and steel framed seats, there were no surfaces available for panelling. In an effort to provide some decor, painted pinstripe borders created the impression of panelled walls. The floors consisted of a slatted surface to prevent the accumulation of water during wet weather; the primary floor a "Monolith" cement used by the Pullman company for the floors of railroad cars. As the open ends of the vestibules permitted the entry of rain and snow, rubber flooring was applied in those areas.

The first cars arrived in the summer of 1904. Operating components were installed at the 147th Street shop, after which they were inspected by domestic and foreign railroad experts. A sensation in the industry press, the cars were accorded substantial space in the general press as well. All three hundred were equipped with motors, the fleet replacing a cancelled order for a like number of Composite cars. When the subway opened with gala civic celebrations on October 27, 1904, one hundred and three steel cars were available for service. The balance of the primary order was completed by the end of the year. The additional order for one hundred was completed in the Spring of 1905,

A triumph for Gibbs, the builder, and the Interborough, the new cars changed forever the precepts of rail car construction. A subsequent order was delivered to the Long Island Rail Road to serve the new electrification, the world's first conversion of an entire operating division from steam to electric propulsion. One Interborough car was loaned to the Long Island in order that the road's shopmen could familiarize themselves with the structure of the car. The tooling and concepts were also used to produce a line of equipment which was exported to London. The Pennsylvania railroad also benefitted, as it began constructing steel cars at Altoona in 1907. As for the established car builders, the message was clear: adapt or get out of the rail car business. There were new companies eager to replace them in the new century should they remain wedded to obsolete methods.

As for the A.C.& F. Company, the order proved an entre' into the world of car building. The firm established a lead which made it one of the foremost transit car builders and a leading manufacturer of freight cars. Today, it remains a major freight car builder and also the owner of the nation's largest fleet of leased freight cars. In the interim, it assembled some of the nation's best metal working facilities, a fact which was brought it to the attention of the Atomic Energy Commission several years after World War II. The Commission was seeking a plant with the ability to handle large metal components. Such components were required to form large DeWar flasks (vacuum bottles) for the cryogenic (supercold) liquid hydrogen fuel of the world's first thermonuclear explosive.

The test device was not a practical weapon but a conglomeration of refrigeration machinery, a "fission" bomb "trigger" and other hardware. An A.C.& F. plant proved the only facility equal to the task. The components were fabricated and then shipped in pieces to the Pacific Ocean test site. A notable achievement, even though that particular A.C.& F. product was destined for evaporation in the world's first thermonuclear explosion!

In retrospect, the Interborough's large fleet of Composite cars need not have existed. Given the rapidity with which the three hundred steel cars were completed, there is no doubt that a large steel fleet could have been assembled by the Fall of 1904 had the established builders been interested in achieving true progress. Such was not the case, a fact which was to prove costly to the Interborough in the years ahead.

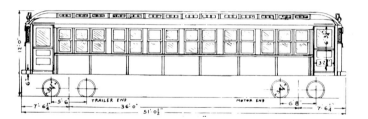

The "Deck Roof" Fleet

The extension of the subway to Brooklyn in 1908 produced an order for fifty additional cars from A.C.& F. in 1907. Essentially similar to the first steel fleet, the cars were delivered the following year. The new fleet incorporated changes which were the result of operating experience. While vestibule boarding was adequate on railroad cars, subway traffic during the rush hours was such that trains were delayed at stations while passengers shoved through the cramped vestibules. The optimal solution would have eliminated vestibules entirely in favor of direct entries into the cars. That approach was obviated by the dangerous gaps which would have been encountered at station platforms constructed on sharp curves.

Thus vestibules were retained but were wider on the new cars. The cumbersome sliding doors between the vestibule and the interior of the car were eliminated. A sliding door was placed acrossthe opening at the outer end of the vestibule. Termed a "storm" door, (a designation still used to describe the end doors of subway cars,) it prevented the entry of wind and weather thus making the vestibule a space available for standing passengers. A pair of folding doors created a motorman's cab at the right side of the vestibule.

The vestibules at the ends of trains were still not used for access as they were generally beyond the platform end. Though open to the interior of the car, Interborough policy forbade standees in the vestibules at the ends of the train, allegedly a safety precaution in the remote event of a collision, It also allowed the end doors to be left open for summertime ventilation. That policy remained in effect until the dissolution of the company in 1940.

Similar in most respects to the earlier steel cars, the new fleet incorporated some variations. Provision was made for the installation of a door at the center of the car in place of the transverse seats. The most obvious difference was the roof clerestory which did not taper down to the end of the car but ended at the vestibule bulkhead. As a result, the area above the vestibules formed a flat "deck" which led to the designation "Deck Roof Motors" for those cars, all of which were equipped with motors.

The original steel cars were them termed "Gibbs" cars even though both steel models were constructed under the Gibbs patents. The Deck Roof fleet was most probably the first to abandon the Tuscan Red and Burnt Orange paint scheme in favor of a dank, utilitarian paint. The result of operating experience that demonstrated the futility of bright colors in the grimy subway tunnels, the new color may have been introduced experimentally on some of the later Gibbs cars.

Excess!

Although there had been concern that the ridership might not be sufficient to assure the profit potential of the subway, it was overcrowded on the first day. As time passed, the excessive crowds delayed trains and became a safety concern. A variety of efforts were developed to improve passenger movement. Station names were added to the support columns, wooden signs were added to walls at the ends of the stations. Large signs were suspended from the ceilings of stations with island platforms as some such locations lacked name tablets. In those that did, the tablets were often obscured by trains. At other locations, large illuminated signs were mounted just beyond the platform for passengers in the portions of the end car which stopped beyond the platform.

A second set of metal plate destination signs was added to each car to supplement the original set. At least one car was fitted with an experimental roof-mounted electric sign on the front, but the results did not warrant installation on the entire fleet. With the exception of the latter, all those measures improved passenger movement but it was obvious that more substantial efforts were required to cope with the overload.

THE EXIGENCIES OF URBAN TRANSIT

While the railroad coach layout was acceptable for service on elevated lines, it proved inadequate for the dense traffic of the subway. Given the assumption that vestibules had to be retained, the only alternative involved additional side doors. Such doors had been incorporated into some elevated cars in both Brooklyn and Boston.

While there was a consensus on the need for direct access to the car interior, there was a divergence of opinion as to the ideal location of such doors. Bion J. Arnold, a railway and electrical expert with nationwide credentials, favored a scheme which required minimal alterations to the structural frame of the cars. In that scenario, two additional doors were to be added to each side of the car in a position adjoining the door pockets of the vestibule doors. Marked "Exit," the new doors were to be used by passengers exiting from the car interior. The original vestibule doors were to be used by entering passengers and were marked "Entrance." The scheme was favored by the Public Service Commission, the regulatory agency which had assumed supervision of the Interborough in 1907. Though curious, it had some precedent. Boston had acquired elevated cars with a center door which was used for exit, the entrance provided by the usual end platforms.

The Interborough preferred a single door at the center of the car, a scheme for which provision had been made in the Deck Roof cars. Test trains were modified according to both schemes. In mid-February, 1909, the train with Arnold's scheme entered service. Subsequently, the Interborough concept was tested. Although the Interborough scheme required substantial structural reinforcement and was not operable at some curved platforms, it entailed less modification and did not require riders to obey signs!

The additional doors proved a boon to service, effecting a 35% reduction in station dwell (standing) time. The entire fleet was modified according to the Interborough scheme as Arnold's plan was cancelled. Arnold disagreed, penning a long letter of disappointment in the trade press. As the program developed, the improvement in service was such that the Commission directed the Interborough to operate center door cars at all hours (not just rush hours) during the transition period.

Operating handles mounted beneath the end windows of the cars were connected mechanically to a pneumatic operating device on the new doors. Unlike the original vestibule doors which closed against air-filled rubber bumpers (intended to prevent injury from closing doors,) the new doors introduced the first mechanical safety device. A large cuff at the edge of the door enclosed a device which halted the closing cycle in the event the door encountered an obstruction.

The heavy mechanical levers were retained on the vestibule doors despite their proven record of crippling injury to the guards. In operating practice, each guard was responsible not only for the vestibule doors adjoining his location but also for the center door of the car to his right. The end guard was responsible for the center doors of both adjoining cars. The center doors were not operable at locations with sharp curves, or points where the center doors of the end cars were beyond the platforms.

FURTHER MODIFICATIONS

The center door program proved a resounding success, enabling the operation of more trains. Reduction of the headways between 40 MPH express trains required either expensive modifications to the signal system or improved braking. As a result, the entire subway car fleet was equipped with a new electropneumatic system (Westinghouse Air Brake AMRE ME-21.) Similar to the original system, it utilized an electric circuit to effect instantaneous application and release of the brakes throughout the train.

The improvement in performance was significant. Field tests by engineers of the Westinghouse Air Brake Company determined that the new system could stop a ten car train moving at 40 MPH in 20 seconds within a distance of 700'. By comparison, the original system required 40 seconds and 1290' to stop a train of only eight cars. The figures for "emergency stops" were even more impressive. The former system required 22 seconds and 625' to stop an eight car train traveling at 40 MPH. The new system reduced those figures to 11 seconds and 350' for a ten car train. In point of fact, the new system posted a gain in braking performance of more than 50% given that the figures included two additional cars. Thus it was possible to operate trains on reduced headways without expensive signal modification. Furthermore, the uniform (as opposed to serial) braking action reduced substantially the wear on couplings, wheels and rails.

As time passed, the cars were modified with "Hedley" anticlimbers on the end sills. Named for Interborough General Superintendent (and later President) Frank Hedley, the device consisted of steel flanges which would interlock with those of the next car during the end compression of a collision to prevent "telescoping," the crashing of one car through another. The original link and pin "Van Dorn" couplers were replaced with a "tightlock" design which improved performance and connected the air brake lines automatically.

The "indication" circuit was an innovation introduced on cars built after 1909. Earlier cars contained gongs which were sounded in succession by each guard from rear to front to inform the motorman that the doors were closed. A clumsy method known informally as "passing the bells," it was supplanted by electrical contacts on all the doors. Positive closure of all the side doors established electrical continuity in the indication circuit throughout the train which then lighted an "indication" lamp in the motorman's operating cab. Indication circuits were added to the existing cars to assure operational compatibility with the newer rolling stock.

The electrical system was not only faster, it was silent. The gongs were subject to misinterpretation when sounded by the crews of trains on adjacent tracks. It may be surmised, however, that the new technique failed to meet with full approval. The fixture containing the indicating light at the operator's position became known euphemistically as the "monkey box." Be that as it may, the indication concept has been an axiom of transit practice ever since.

Yet another modification was made in 1910, as much a delight to the passengers of that era as is air conditioning today. The original tunnels of the Interborough were plagued by excessive heat due to the lack of ventilating grates and layers of tar and felt waterproofing. A variety of cooling schemes were introduced; reduced nighttime lighting, small fans on station columns, ventilation chambers with louvers actuated by the draft from passing trains, even an Artesian well cooling system. After five years of discussion and surveys, ceiling mounted "windmill" fans were installed in the cars in 1910!

While the commentators of the 1904 period were impressed with the lighting of the stations and cars, the interior lighting of the Composite fleet was far from bright. The scratch brushed aluminum ceiling of the steel cars provided a brighter appearance but the ten candlepower lamps left something to be desired. With the continuing improvement of incandescent lamps, sixteen candlepower bulbs were installed after the subway opened. In 1911, thirty-two candlepower lamps were substituted, doubling the light and producing favorable comment.

STANDARDIZATION

Three hundred and twenty five additional steel cars were acquired from three builders during 1910 and 1911. American Car & Foundry supplied 110, while two newcomers, the Pressed Steel Car Company and the Standard Steel Car Company, supplied 40 and 175 units respectively. As all of the new cars were equipped with motors, scores of Composite motor cars were converted to trailers, more than two hundred being completed over several years.

While the new cars incorporated the revised vestibules, center doors, electropneumatic brakes, indication light circuits and other developments, the bodies incorporated new techniques of steel construction. Riveted plates over a steel frame were utilized without the heavy side girders of the Gibbs design. Thus the entire car was steel and wood was eliminated from the roof and interior fittings. Influenced by Frank Hedley, the cars were termed "Hedley Motors." They were also called "Battleships" due to the steel plate construction. As it developed, the body became the "standard" for the Interborough, as the design was utilized for more than 1600 constructed over the next fifteen years.

Despite the new construction techniques and some changes in the electrical components, the new cars retained the heavy, man-crippling manual levers for the vestibule doors. As before, the center doors were controlled by the small secondary lever and pneumatic mechanism.

The new cars permitted the operation of longer trains on more frequent intervals. The first six car locals were operated on October 24, 1910, the first ten car expresses on January 23, 1911. Ten car express trains and six car locals became the standard, an increase of two and one respectively from the peak hour standard established in 1904. The increase was facilitated by the modification of platforms at most stations. In some cases, however, not all of the doors on the end cars could be opened. Overall, the total passenger capacity of the subway during rush hours was increased by a substantial margin.

A serious problem existed at those locations where sharp curves prevented the use of the center doors on some or most of the cars. Such restrictions were most acute at 14th Street and Brooklyn Bridge, two stations at which traffic was heavy and delays frequent. A "gap filler" of sliding metal gratings was installed at locations where hazardous gaps existed. Operated by pneumatic power, the device slid out against the side of the cars to prevent accidents, then retracted as the train started to move. An extensive installation was completed at 14th Street in February, 1914, a simpler installation was added at Brooklyn Bridge.

After acquisition of the Hedley motors in 1911, the Interborough fleet numbered more than 1,150 cars. As it developed, that number was about to double. Rapid expansion of the city required construction of additional subway lines and both the Interborough and the Brooklyn Rapid Transit Company contracted for the construction, equipment and operation of new lines. The Interborough tripled in size, the expansion part of a program termed the "Dual Contracts" of 1913.

SECOND PHASE:

EXPANSION THROUGHOUT THE BOROUGHS

NEW TECHNOLOGY AND SPECIALIZED REQUIREMENTS

Substantial advances had been made in rapid transit car technology by the time of the Dual Contracts. Although the Interborough never revised the standard body design, substantial changes were made in the operating components of later cars. One of the earliest developments was the use of electrical relays to advance the motor circuits automatically. Such "automatic acceleration" had been in use for years on many properties. In point of fact, it had been installed on the Gibbs cars built for the Long Island Rail Road in 1905. Similar equipment was utilized on the elevated cars of the Brooklyn Rapid Transit Company.

Although the electromechanical components required for automatic acceleration were more complex, such systems reduced component wear and power consumption, provided a smoother ride, and were simpler to operate. By the time cars were required for the expansion, both General Electric and Westinghouse had perfected automatic acceleration control which would operate on battery power. New, reliable batteries had been developed which guaranteed control function regardless of the availability of third rail power to each car. Such low voltage circuits simplified the design of the control system, while reducing the bulk and complexity of the components. The cumbersome line voltage "bus" jumpers were no longer required. The batteries also made practical the use of secondary "emergency" interior lights which illuminated auto-

matically whenever third rail power was interrupted.

Improved air brakes had also been developed. Whereas the AMRE brake was essentially an electrical actuating mechanism imposed on an automatic air brake system, the Westinghouse Air Brake Company's AMUE ME-23 brake was innovative. Developed to meet the needs of rapid transit, interurban and commuter rail operators, the system combined the air and electric features so as to function as a unified system.

The new Interborough cars did not incorporate the electropneumatic door control systems which had been adopted by the Brooklyn Rapid Transit Company and other operators. They did, however, eliminate the brutal manual door operating levers from future cars. Instead, the pneumatic mechanism was installed on all doors. Thus all the side doors could be controlled from the small levers located beneath the end windows of the car. The revision was less than altruistic, however, as the new approach enabled one man to operate all the side doors of a pair of cars. Thus, guards were no longer required at each and every pair of vestibules. The crew requirement for a six car local was reduced from five to three while that of a ten car express was reduced from nine to five. Quite a reduction in an era when wages were starting to increase due to increasing organization efforts on the part of labor!

Curiously, the Interborough chose to ignore other trends within the industry. While fabric roll signs were becoming standard, the company continued the use of painted metal signs in brackets on a side window. Each sign set included a large tray with a complete set of signs for all services and destinations.

As it stood, the Interborough did not adopt any of the new technologies immediately. Instead, the company chose to pioneer the new developments on a small order of twelve cars supplied by the Pressed Steel Car in 1915.

The small order was acquired to initiate service through the "Steinway" tunnel which connected Long Island City, Queens with East 42nd Street, Manhattan. Constructed for trolley cars, revised plans utilized it as the link between new rapid transit routes in Northwest Queens and a crosstown route in mid-Manhattan. Although modified for subway service, the gradients of the tunnel were such that the existing motor cars might have encountered difficulty in maintaining schedule speed. It was determined that no unpowered trailer cars should operate through the tunnel and that the motor cars should have a gear ratio which would improve performance.

As the initial order for equipment was to be small, it was decided that the cars would serve as a "test bed" for new developments. Thus the cars became the first "Low Voltage" cars on the roster, a designation indicating battery controls and automatic acceleration. (Prior motor cars were designated High Voltage cars; the subclasses being Gibbs, Deck Roof, or Standard-also known as Hedley or Battleship.) Furthermore, those first Low Voltage cars were subclassed "Steinway" for the special motor gearing.

Service through the Steinway tunnel commenced on June 22, 1915. After one year of service, the new technology was adopted with one exception. That was the use of an "electric portion" on the coupler which connected all control circuits automatically. As the control circuits were limited to battery power, the placement of several circuits of different polarity and potential in such close proximity did not present a problem. Whatever the reasons, electric portions were not adopted by the Interborough. Although the devices became standard throughout the transit industry, the Interborough remained an exception. The electric portions were then removed from the test cars. In all other aspects, the test cars set new standards: battery powered controls with automatic acceleration and the AMUE brake which became the norm.

With the new lines of the Dual Contracts expansion program underway, hundreds of new cars were required. Before that need was addressed, the company finally developed a means by which the wooden Composite cars could be removed from the subway.

THE GREAT TRADE

The operation of the Composite cars in the subway tunnels had been a source of controversy since the inception of service. Although substantial time, effort and expense had been invested in the effort to make them fire and crash resistant, more than twenty-three had been retired due to various mishaps. In early 1915, Frank Hedley announced that a decision had been reached which would remove the cars from subway service and mollify the public, press, and regulatory authorities. It so happened that the Manhattan elevated network was also being expanded under a certificate which was a corollary agreement to the Dual Contracts. Additional rolling stock was required but there was little interest in purchasing more of the standard Manhattan elevated cars. Under the Hedley scheme, the Composite cars were to be modified for service on the Manhattan elevated lines.

The modification program included the removal of ceiling fans, the replacement of the "subway type" (upper sash movable) with "elevated type" (lower sash movable) windows, and the installation of headlights. The altered Composite car bodies were fitted with new lightweight trucks fabricated at the Manhattan Company's 129th Street shops. Termed the "Maximum Traction" type, each truck contained only one traction motor, the wheels on the powered axle having a larger diameter than those on the unpowered axle. Thus the weight of the motors was distributed, an important consideration given the load limitations of the elevated structure.

The trade yielded a total of 477 new Composite elevated cars, all of which were equipped as motor cars with AMUE brakes and tightlock couplers. The modified Composite fleet was not compatible with the Manhattan elevated fleet owing to differences in the couplers, motor controls, and air brakes. The Composite fleet was restricted to service on the new express tracks of the Second and Third Avenue elevated lines and also on the reconstructed City Hall branch. Return trips over the local tracks had to be made without passengers due to the weight limitations of the local tracks which had not been rebuilt. That unusual operation did not pose a problem given the volume of trains returning opposite to the prevailing direction of traffic. In fact, it probably expedited the return movement.

The Flivvers

New steel car bodies of the standard 1910 type arrived from the Pullman Company and were mounted upon the trucks salvaged from the Composite fleet. The swap occurred on temporary trackage at the New York Central yard in the Highbridge section of the Bronx. The operating hardware salvaged from the Composite cars was then installed on the new cars at the Interborough shops. A total of 478 steel cars were created by the trade. The bulk were configured as replacement trailer cars for the 1904-1911 steel "High Voltage" motor cars (Gibbs, Deck Roof, and Standard) but there was also a significant variation.

Sufficient motors and controls were salvaged from the Composite cars to equip one hundred twenty four cars, the balance of the original Composite motor cars having been converted to trailers during the fleet expansion of 1908-1911. Curiously, the new steel motor cars were not equipped with the old High Voltage electrical system. Although there is some question as to whether or not it was installed and removed in the early 1920s, the cars were oddities during the latter four decades of operation. With a Low Voltage

control system that was at least similar to that adopted for other new cars, the fleet retained the old AMRE ME-21 brake system.

As a result, those motors plus fifty four similar trailers were incompatible with either of the two standard Interborough fleets. Furthermore, the odd units worked well only in certain combinations, a restriction which was observed strictly. Normally operated on the Seventh Avenue-Bronx Park express, the cars were stored at hours when train consists were divided in Brooklyn. Under such circumstances, there was no guarantee that the same cars would be reassembled. The failure to do so could result in poor operation. Officially "Low Voltage AMRE" cars, the fleet was termed "Flivvers" by the crews, probably a reference to the rough riding autos of the period.

Such complexity begs the question as to why the entire fleet was not standardized around the new battery powered controls with automatic acceleration. While that would have entailed the purchase and installation of batteries, and modifications to the control system, it would have yielded substantial benefits. Operation and crew training would have been simplified, parts inventories would have been reduced, and repair procedures streamlined.

Such a move would have eliminated the need for the special signals on each side of every third rail section break on all the lines, both original and new. That change would have yielded a substantial reduction in capital expenditures for signals on the new lines and eliminated all future expenditures for the maintenance of section break signals. While the most logical explanation is the cost of conversion, there is also the possibility that inbred resistance to change played a role. Certainly, the retention of steel plate signs, the absence of electric portions on couplers and the use of kerosene running lamps on cars with batteries would indicate such an explanation. It is also possible that the Flivvers were the test bed for such a conversion and that the results discouraged any large scale modification.

By contrast, the Interborough invested substantial sums on improvements to the original signals and Interlocking plants. Similar improvements were made on the Interborough's Manhattan elevated division. Financial constraints had pushed the Interborough to the edge of insolvency during World War I and improvements to the system's physical plant were probably assessed in terms of cost/benefit. The signal improvements increased both capacity and safety. Heavy investments in the power generating and distribution system were essential if the potential inherent in the expanded system was to be realized. By comparison, it may have been determined that expensive alterations to a large fleet of cars of proven reliability was not cost effective.

THE LOW VOLTAGE FLEET

The first large order of Interborough subway cars for the new lines involved three hundred and eleven Low Voltage cars built by the Pullman Company. Equipped with automatic acceleration, battery control circuits and AMUE brakes, they set the standard for the future. Delivered in 1917, seventy one were geared for Steinway service, the balance for mainline service. The mainline cars included the first Low Voltage trailer cars as the motor/trailer ratio was a staple of Interborough practice. With the elimination of the line voltage "bus" supplying third rail power throughout the train, the Low Voltage trailer cars required third rail shoes. Unlike motor cars, the trailers carried shoes on only one truck.

A subsequent order for 477 cars was completed by the Pullman Company in 1920. Of the latter, seventy five were Steinway motor cars, the balance included both motor and trailer cars for mainline service. One hundred additional mainline trailers were delivered by the Pullman Company in 1922.

Rapid urban development produced severe overcrowding on the new subway lines within a few years. Trapped by rising debt and demands for improved services, the company agreed to purchase additional cars. In 1924, the American Car & Foundry Company supplied two hundred fifty cars, in two groups. The "100 Lot" involved mainline motor cars, the "150 Lot" included twenty five Steinway motor cars. The delivery of the cars enabled two significant service improvements. First, the use of shuttles of elevated cars (Composites) on the outer portions of new subway extensions ceased. Such segments (outside of tunnels) served areas in which development was sparse and traffic minimal. Passengers in those areas enjoyed through service after the new cars were delivered. The second improvement was a substantial reduction in "shortlining," the turning of alternate trains at points prior to the end of the line as a means of increasing midtown service.

The "150 Lot" cars of 1925 completed the acquisition of subway cars for the new lines of the Interborough Rapid Transit Company. It also marked the last delivery of cars with vestibules. Beset by financial difficulties, the company was unable to expand the fleet. When the Queens line to Carona was extended to Flushing in 1928, the need for additional Steinway motor cars was filled by converting thirty of the 1915 trailer cars which consisted of new Pullman bodies on trucks salvaged from the Composite fleet.

MULTIPLE UNIT DOOR CONTROL

Although the Interborough had been slow to adopt many new practices, the directors were eager to reduce operating expense wherever possible. Automatic, coin operated turnstiles were installed after lengthy negotiations with state regulators. In 1920, the Interborough introduced the concept of Multiple Unit Door Control. That scheme involved electrical control of electropneumatic door engines on every side door. One man could operate the doors of an entire train although the regulatory officials specified two men on trains of ten cars.

Thus the company replaced the phalanx of guards with a single "conductor." Ten car trains included a "rear guard." Operational safety was enhanced by the placement of the door controls at the outer sides of the ends of the car. The crewmen stood upon steel plates at the edge of the car, the elevation providing a view above the passengers and along the length of the train. Passenger safety was further assured by the presence of a red "guard" light on the side of each car which illuminated whenever any side door on that car was not closed completely. Accident claims were reduced substantially. As before, positive closure of all side doors was confirmed by the illumination of the indicating lamp at the motorman's position.

An additional safety measure was incorporated into to the new doors. Unlike the mechanical linkage which halted the closing action of the earlier pneumatic doors, a mechanism in the cuff on the doors caused the doors to reopen. In rush hours, it became virtually impossible to get the doors closed at crowded stations. Burly "platform men" were assigned to such locations to shove passengers into the cars to permit the doors to close!

Multiple Unit Door Control was installed on the Low Voltage cars and Flivvers during 1920, new cars being equipped upon delivery. In 1923, 266 of the 1910 High Voltage motor cars were so equipped along with 127 High Voltage trailers. With no battery circuit available on the High Voltage fleet, it was necessary to add a small battery for the door circuit. The balance of the 1910 High Voltage motor cars, the remaining trailers and all Gibbs and Deck Roof cars retained the old door control components. At that time, such cars were assigned to locals and shuttles, services which involved trains of only three to five cars staffed by two to four guards.

MINOR MODIFICATIONS

Minor alterations were made to the entire fleet during the 1920s. New third rail shoes replaced the original design in 1921. Providing improved power collection at high speed, the design was installed after extensive studies with current oscillographs. The seat backs which had been installed near the center doors as a means of directing the movement of passengers had proven an impediment. After a test train without the barriers was operated in early 1929, they were removed from the entire fleet. Likewise, folding seats at the center doors (intended for use during off peak operation) which were used rarely if ever, were removed in subsequent years. Finally, the slatted flooring was replaced by solid material.

THE LAST DECADE

With the Company in the throes of financial disaster, the loss of traffic during the Depression led to bankruptcy in 1932. The Interborough was placed under the administration of Thomas E. Murray, an industrialist, philanthropist and civic leader active in both Manhattan and Brooklyn. The major thrust of his management was focused on the need to keep the vital transit network operating until the situation was resolved. Although it was obvious that the only practical solution involved a transfer of the Interborough's assets to the city, Murray's eight year tenure saw not only reliable service but improvements as well.

While there were no funds for new car technology, the company did manage to develop an experimental "soundproof" car in 1933. The noise reduction was accomplished by modifications to the vestibules and the installation of blowers which permitted the closure of the windows during normal operation. A safety mechanism released the windows automatically in the event of equipment failure.

The car met with the approval of both riders and officials, Health Commissioner Shirley Wynne in particular. She noted that the innovation would help reduce nervous tension and blood pressure during the stressful daily commute. Six cars were tested at the end of the year but financial constraints terminated the effort at that time.

One hundred and twenty five of the original steel Gibbs motor cars were equipped with Multiple Unit Door Control in 1936. One hundred, and sixty three High Voltage trailer cars were also equipped at that time. As a result, the total number of High Voltage cars with Multiple Unit Door Control was such that no Interborough train required more than two guards. The remaining manual door cars were utilized as "pilot" cars at the ends of trains, all the other cars having multiple unit door control. Thus it was possible to position the crewmen such that each could operate one manual door car, and the balance electrically.

Though beneficial to he struggling company, the new "pilot car" practice increased the burden on the conductors and guards. While operating the manual vestibule door levers of adjoining cars was a brutal task, the use of both arms did provide a certain anatomical symmetry. Under such circumstances, the guard could use his body weight advantageously. With the pilot car arrangement, only one lever was involved, the guard manipulating the lever in an unbalanced manner. As a result, the physiological requirement on the operating arm was greater and the rate of crippling injuries increased. Thus, the guards tended to open only the pneumatic powered center door whenever the traffic was not heavy, thus sparing their arms, backs, and internal organs.

A FINAL VARIATION

With the Interborough company in bankruptcy, studies of light-weight steel cars for the Manhattan elevated lines were terminated. Indeed, John Madison, the head of the Interborough's car design team, had left the company in the late 1920s to direct the car development program for the City's new Independent Subway. However, once Flushing Meadow was designated the site of a World's Fair, years of transit improvement demands by northwest Queens groups bore fruit. Provision had been made for express service on both Interborough lines in Queens but only limited track had been installed and much of that was used to store surplus Manhattan elevated cars. In view of the financial situation of the Interborough, it was decided that the city would fund the necessary improvements as part of investment in the Fair. As the operator of the Independent Subway, the City Board of Transportation maintained a staff of experienced rapid transit engineers.

Fifty new cars were required for the express service to the Fair. The Board's engineers hesitated to approve more cars of the Interborough's obsolete vestibule design, a configuration which had been retained because of the sharp curves at some mainline stations. On the other hand, it was not certain that the Interborough would become a city property. In that case, the time and expense of the Board staff would have been expended on a project of sole benefit to a private corporation.

Once again it was time for compromise. The Board's engineers modified the standard car by relocating the doors to provide passenger access similar to that of the cars built for the Independent subway. Vestibules were eliminated. For the first time, Interborough motormen enjoyed the comfort of an enclosed operating cab instead of the drafty and dusty end vestibule. The marker lights were recessed into the front of the car. Fabric roll signs finally appeared on Interborough cars, but only at the end of the car.
The standard railroad clerestory was eliminated, replaced by a solid curved roof into which "box" ventilators were inserted.

Innovation ended there. The basic features of the standard Interborough car was retained. Large columns marked the positions where the vestibule bulkheads were found in the standard cars. Longitudinal passenger seats and a window were located opposite the motorman's cab, a feature of the Independent cars. In this case, however, the seat was bordered by the aforementioned column. The signs on the side of the car retained the antiquated metal plates. Kerosene running lamps were also retained. Some changes were made in the electrical components, the most obvious of which was in the door circuits.

The new units used electrical contacts connected by "Koil-Kord" of the type common to residential telephone handsets. More than one rider was puzzled by what appeared to be telephone wires swaying under the glass windows of the door pockets as the train moved down the track! The propulsion, braking, and control systems were common to those of the Steinway Low Voltage cars.

All in all, the cars represented what engineers would term a "quick and dirty" solution to an immediate need. Many of the decisions were cost-driven. Only one cab was equipped with motorman's controls, a departure from standard Interborough practice. The other cab was fitted with a longitudinal passenger seat. Likewise, only one end was equipped with conductor's controls, a variation from former Interborough practice. The fifty car order was placed with the St. Louis Car Company and delivered in 1938. After installation of operating hardware at the 147th Street shop, the cars were placed in service on the Flushing line.

The new "World's Fair" cars operated in trains with the standard Steinway type equipment in both express and local service on the Flushing line. As it happened, the need for yet more cars was filled by the transfer of some standard Low Voltage cars to Flushing service. Though not equipped with Steinway gearing, the cars performed adequately when operated without trailers. When used in Queens they were confined to trains of like equipment to prevent any mismatch with Steinway cars during starting and acceleration.

The "World's Fair" cars received only minimal notice in the press, most media attention being directed toward the new "World's Fair Railroad" spur of the Independent subway. The IRT "World's Fair" cars received more notice after they were transferred to mainline service a decade later. The reconstruction of parts of the Flushing line received more substantial attention. The Willets Point Boulevard local station was reconstructed as a large, three platform express complex to serve the Fair.

The approach tracks to the Carona storage yard and inspection shed were modified and an upper level express "flyover" was added to the 111th Street station to expedite service. Bidirectional block signaling was installed on the express track for the new service.

FINALE'

Be that as it may, the end of the Interborough company was at hand. After much political rhetoric, terms were reached which met the demands of all the parties concerned. At 12:01 am on June 12, 1940, the assets of the Interborough company were transferred to the City, the operation to become the IRT Division of the New York City Transit System. A special edition of the company's public relations newsletter, the "Subway Sun", featured a caricature of Murray handing a toy subway to Mayor Fiorello La Guardia.

UNDER CITY OPERATION

THE EARLY YEARS

Few changes were forthcoming immediately. An experimental, "Air-Vented" train was tested in 1941, an outgrowth of the earlier soundproof experiments. Then World War II inflicted substantial injury to the physical plant of the nation's railroads and transit systems. Shortages of manpower and the rationing of critical materials required continued use of components which should have been replaced. Moreover, strict rationing of motor fuel and tires placed heavy traffic on the subway system. Then a postwar economic boom burdened the abused and aging physical plant.

INITIAL CHANGES

The Board initiated substantial rehabilitation plans at the end of the war. The first impact of those plans came in the form of new cars during the summer of 1948. With new propulsion and braking systems, the cars posted substantial improvements in running time. Introduced on the Flushing line, the cars delighted Queens riders. Two hundred and fifty new cars displaced all the Steinway cars from the Flushing line by mid-1949. After the Astoria line was transferred to the BMT division, all the Steinway cars were reassigned to the Lexington Avenue Local to provide increased service.

One little noted event of that period occurred on April 28, 1950. On that evening, the last Composite cars were retired from express service on the Third Avenue elevated line. In 1951, the door reopening feature was finally removed from the cars of the old Interborough Company. Signs reading "Hands Off- Will Not Reopen If Held By You" were posted on the doors. The cuffs at the edge of the doors remained, however, a puzzle to younger riders who had never witnessed the reopening feature in action.

At the same time, the Board was contemplating the future of the entire subway system. There was particular concern for the older equipment of the Interborough as consulting engineers recommended that cars should be retired at the age of fifty years.

MORE CHANGES AND NEW ADMINISTRATION

By 1952, the age of the fleet was such that the availability of cars for peak service was threatened. As a stopgap measure, twenty of the 1915 High Voltage trailer cars were converted to" Blind" motor cars without cabs. The Board of Transportation was replaced by the New York City Transit Authority in mid-1953. In 1954, the Authority contracted with the St. Louis Car Company for the first cars which would initiate the modernization of the IRT fleet. At that time, the ideal replacement age for rolling stock was set at forty years. It was reduced subsequently to thirty five, a figure which was confirmed by the consulting firm of Coverdale & Colpitts during a system wide survey in 1959-60.

In 1955, the Transit Authority was reorganized and Charles L. Patterson became Chairman. Patterson took office with a mandate from elected officials to operate the subway system on a self-sustaining basis, only capital expenditures were to be borne by the city taxpayers. A career railroader who had observed first hand the efficiencies inherent in the use of modern technology, Patterson espoused an immediate modernization of the Interborough fleet.

PHASEOUT

As the availability of the IRT fleet continued to decline, eight more 1915 High Voltage trailer cars were converted to blind motors. The first new cars (R-17 class) entered service on the Pelham line in October, 1955, initiating the replacement of the Interborough High Voltage fleet. Old cars with the brutal manual doors were the first to go, those with multiple unit doors being retired later. Subsequent deliveries of seven hundred new cars acquired under two contracts (R-21/R-22) retired the High Voltage cars by the Fall of 1958. Among the last to operate were three Gibbs cars nearly fifty four years old.

In view of the fact that they were destined to remain on the property for several years, the Low Voltage fleet was equipped with electric running lights during the 1950s. The last kerosene lamps were eliminated with the retirement of the High Voltage cars in 1958, the change freeing a total of 58 men for other tasks.

A total of one thousand, four hundred and ten new cars (R-26/28/29/33/36) were delivered between the Fall of 1959(R-26) and the Summer of 1964 (R-36.) Replacement of the Low Voltage fleet began in 1960. The last Flivver cars were retired by the Spring of 1962. New cars then replaced the mainline and Steinway Low Voltage cars, the last being removed from the Lexington-Jerome Line by Christmas of 1963. A few remaining cars continued to operate on the Seventh Avenue-Lenox line until the late winter of 1964. The Bowling Green-South Ferry shuttle continued to operate with old cars until the mid-summer of 1964.

The end of an era. *HGF*

THE END

The end of the Interborough fleet came in 1969, a watershed year in world, local and transit history. It was the year of the first manned moon landing, and a surprise world series victory by the New York Mets. The last of the BMT "Standard" cars were retired that summer. It was also the year in which the last true wooden elevated cars (BMT Q-Type,) the last wooden passenger cars in North America, were retired.

In November,1969 the last Interborough cars were removed from service on the Third Avenue elevated line in the Bronx. Still carrying steel plate signs and other remnants of their roots in the early twentieth century, the entire fleet of 1938 World's Fair Steinways and a few remaining standard Steinways were retired. The Interborough fleet was history.

RETROSPECTIVE

It has been rumored that the bodies of some Composite cars still exist in the Midwest. Sold as surplus during World War II, they were utilized to transport workers at war production plants and also at some Prisoner of War camps. One Gibbs car, #3352, awaits the completion of a restoration effort at the Seashore Trolley Museum in Kennebunkport, Me. Deck Roof car #3662 is stored at the Shore Line Trolley Museum in East Haven, Ct. The latter collection includes standard Low Voltage car #5466.

Four Low Voltage motor cars in operable condition are stored on the property of the transit system. The volunteer effort of a few dedicated historians has restored them to operable condition, an effort which made possible the operation of the cars on the 42nd Street shuttle on the occasion of the 90th anniversary of the first subway. One Low Voltage trailer car (#4902) is displayed at the New York Transit Museum in Brooklyn.

COMPOSITES

The production Composite posed at the Wason car company plant

(top)
On the way to New York City over the high iron!

(BOTTOM)
The first arrivals at 148th Street shop.

The new Composites at the 148th Street yard in 1904 prior to the commencement of subway service [AL/EBW]

A commemorative gift given to the public
from the Rapid transit Rail Road Commission,
shows the first subway car pulled by a former
El steam locomotive to the electrified portion
of the line.
[AL/EBW]

(RIGHT)
The first car 3025 along the Third Avnue El subway connection in the Bronx. *[AL/EBW]*

As more cars arrived, space was at a premium in the unfinished subway. Cars were stored on the Manhattan Valley arch.(Now 125th St,)

3011 at Jewett Car Company plant.
[AL/EBW]

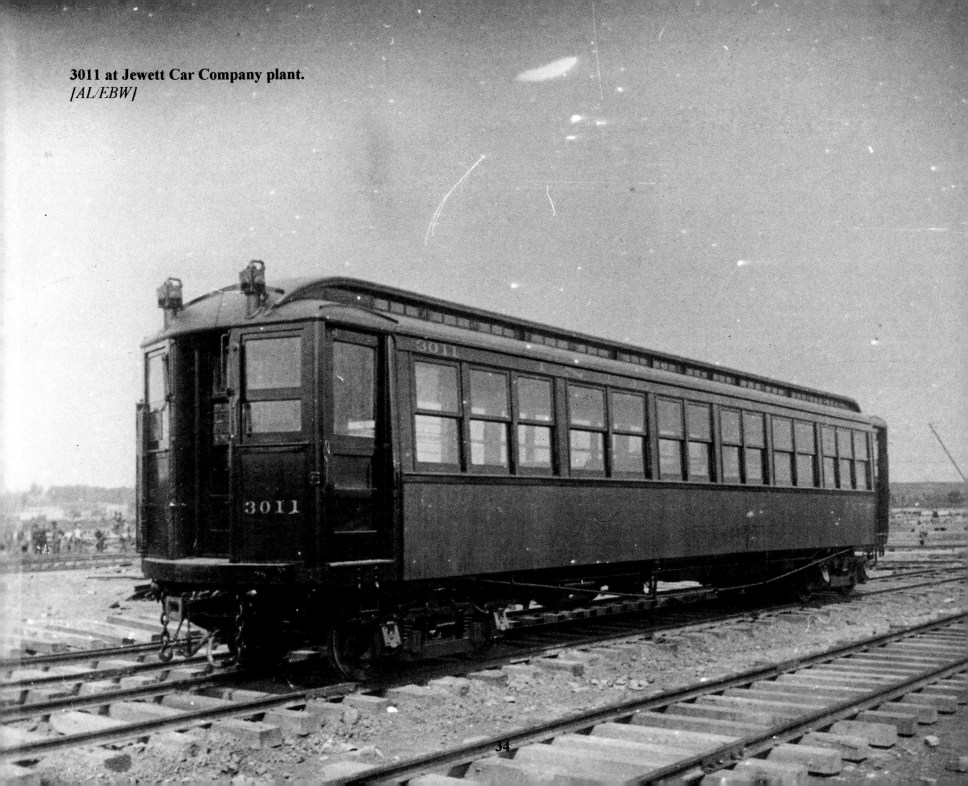

Rows of Composites at 148th Street shop
March 10, 1904.

35

(4532) EQUIP 148 ST & 7 AVE

**Van Cortlandt Park express at Bowling Green
May 15, 1909.** *[AL/EBW]*

City Hall Subway Station, New York.

Belle epoch travel c.1904 smartly
attired New Yorkers board glossy
new Composite cars at the ornate
City Hall station. *[NG]*

INTERBOROUGH
RAPID TRANSIT CO.
SUBWAY DIVISION
GOOD 5 FOR
ONE CONTINUOUS TRIP
5-50-2 D209594

The ticket to ride! A reproduction
of the original IRT ticket.

Interior of production Composite car. *[AL/EBW]*

6-11-1903
(3383) 98 ST Shop
CAR 3341

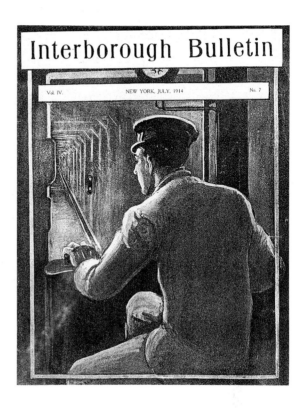

Interborough Bulletin

Vol. IV.   NEW YORK, JULY, 1914   No. 7

Here is a rare picture
of 3341 the original No.#2
John B. McDonald long after
being rebuilt in the IRT
instruction car at 98th St.
Shops of the 3rd. Ave. El.
[AL/EBW]

Manhattan Street (125 St.) Station prior to commencement of public service. *[AL/EBW]*

(BOTTOM)
A proud product of the St Louis Car Company lot #356, here retouched for the companies catalogue in 1904. *[AL/EBW]*

40

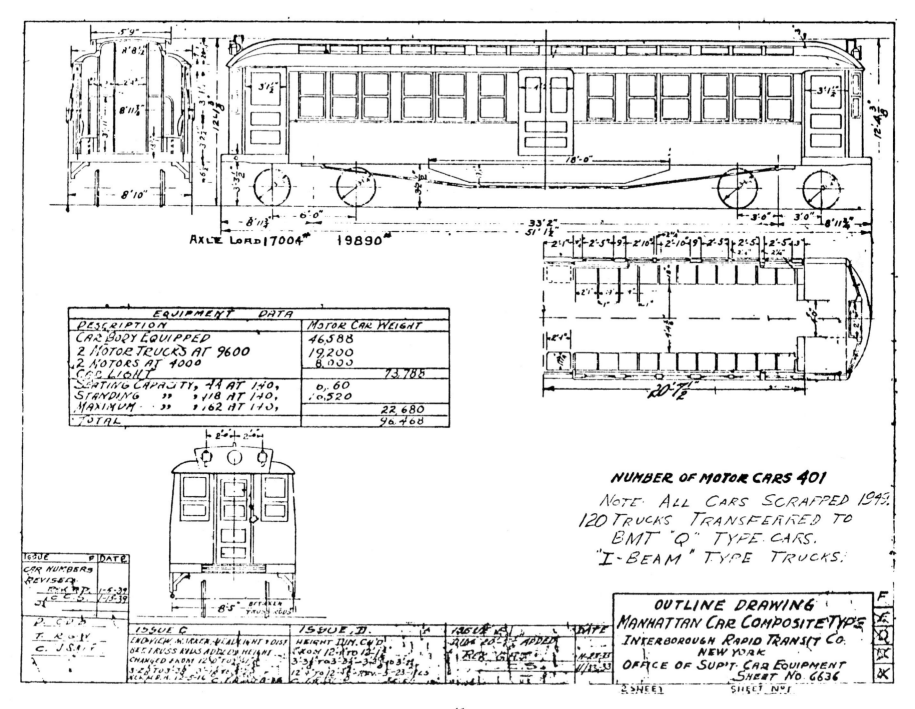

AXLE LOAD 17004#   19890#

EQUIPMENT DATA	
DESCRIPTION	MOTOR CAR WEIGHT
CAR BODY EQUIPPED	46,588
2 MOTOR TRUCKS AT 9600	19,200
2 MOTORS AT 4000	8,000
CAR LIGHT	73,788
SEATING CAPACITY, 44 AT 140,	0, 60
STANDING " , 118 AT 140,	10,520
MAXIMUM " , 162 AT 140,	
	22,680
TOTAL	96,468

NUMBER OF MOTOR CARS 401

NOTE ALL CARS SCRAPPED 1949.
120 TRUCKS TRANSFERRED TO
BMT "Q" TYPE CARS.
"I-BEAM" TYPE TRUCKS.

ISSUE	F	DATE
CAR NUMBERS REVISED.		
F.K.R.P.		1-5-39
C.C.S.		1-15-39
P. CDB		
T. R.G.N.		
C. JSAFF		

ISSUE C	ISSUE D	ISSUE B	DATE
END VIEW MARKER, HEAD LIGHT DIST.	HEIGHT DIM. CHG'D	DIM. 20-7½ ADDED	
DET. TRUSS RODS ADDED ON HEIGHT	FROM 12-4 TO 12-4½	REF. GIVEN	11-27-33
CHANGED FROM 12-6 TO 12-4	3-3½ TO 3-3½ - 3-0 TO 3-1		11-13-33
3-2½ TO 3-1½	12-9 TO 12-8 REV. 5-23-1929		

OUTLINE DRAWING
MANHATTAN CAR COMPOSITE TYPE
INTERBOROUGH RAPID TRANSIT CO.
NEW YORK
OFFICE OF SUP'T CAR EQUIPMENT
SHEET NO 6636

2 SHEET   SHEET N°1

#3322 in elevated service (probably 99 St. yard) *[AL/EBW)*

Experimental mechanical station annunciator in Composite car. *[AL/EBW]*

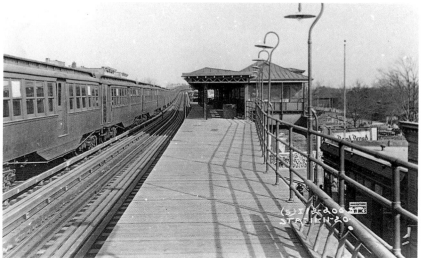

Composite 2129 and others stored at 200 St. On Webster Avenue extension of the Third Ave El Nov. 11, 1920. *[AL/EBW]*

(Top Left)
Subway crowds required the addition of doors at the center of the car. The original leather straps were replaced subsequently by the porcelain coated metal handholds which were a standard for the Interborough. *[AL/EBW]*

Interborough Bulletin

EXPRESS

I.R.T. LEAGUE

IRT

BOUND FOR HEDLEY FIELD..

(Preceding page 44)
3141 in express service on the Third avenue El. At 42nd Street. *[AL/EBW]*
(Preceding page 45)
#2051 heads a 7th Ave through express at 42 St. June 25, 1950. The plethora of operating appliances on the front of the car detail the changes made over the years. From top to bottom-the spot light c1916, the center door operating levers beneath the windows c1911. Adding to the jumble are mismatched safety chains. The end "Storm" door is open, an Interborough practice in the warm weather.

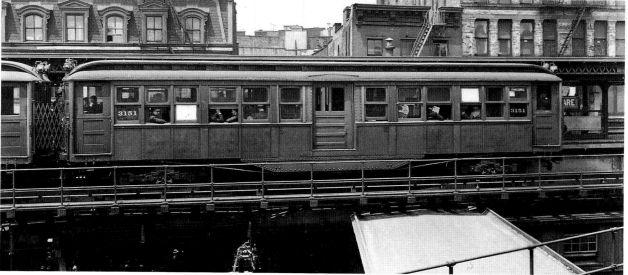

(Opposite page top)
**3000 stored for rush hour service
on center track at 156 St. and Third Ave.**
(Opposite page bottom)
3151 on the Second ave. Express in 1936.
(Top right)
**3306 on inspection at 239 St. yard-White
Plains Road line.**
(Bottom)
**Composite cars on the Polo Grounds
Shuttle.1941**

(Left) **2027 at 34th and Third Ave. On the last run of Composite cars.** *[AL/EBW]*
(Right) **Years of service are visible on 3082 and mates stored for scrap in 1945.**
(Bottom) **2087 off to the scrapper in 1946.** *[AL/EBW]*

Composites hauling war plant workers at the Remington arms plant in 1943. Pulled by a B class Illinois Terminal locomotive.*[GV]*

Composites hauling war plant workers at the Remington arms plant in 1943.*[GV]*

Reincarnated! An old Composite serves as a diner in Farmington Indiana in July 1951. One of a group used during the war to transport war plant workers in Illinois.*[AL/EBW]*

THE END OF WOOD CONSTRUCTION AND THE BEGINNING OF THE STEEL ERA.

(TOP RIGHT)
In a test conducted by the IRT, a steel train impacted a train of composites at low speed with the following results. Another example happened in 1927 when a composite rolled of the unfinished yard lead to the Corona shops. *[AL/EBW]*

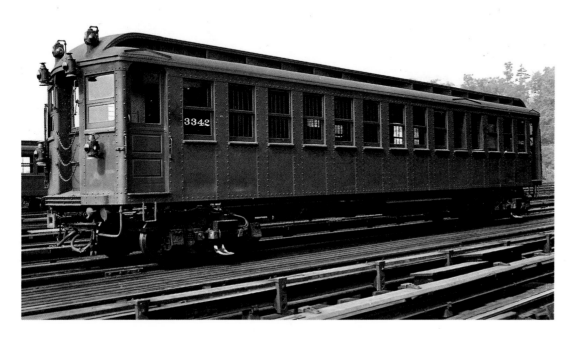

(TOP)
3342 was built by the Altoona shops
of the Pennsyvannia Railroad. It was
the first all steel car but always an oddity
that spent its working career as the IRT
pay car. The well armored car
(LOWER LEFT) is pictured stated at Dyckman
Street in front of sub-station #17. In later
years it is pictured at 148th St. shops. *[AL/EBW]*

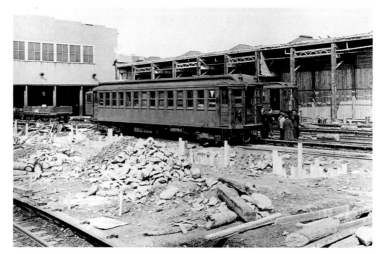

3350

GIBBS CARS

If we match the emotion we get at seeing the latest Hi-speed train set going into service, that same feeling must be akin to what one felt in 1904 looking at these new rapid transit champions of that time. *[AL-EBW]*

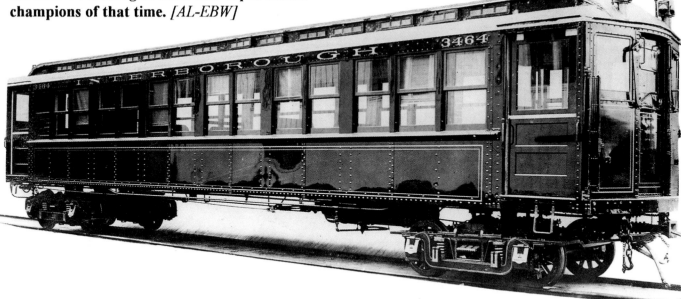

First production steel cars at ACF plant.

(Top)
The interior of the Gibbs car varied little from that of the Composite. The pair of "Merry Widow" sliding doors in the bulk head is clear in this view.[AL/EBW]
(bottom)
3545 at 147 Street shop.[GV]
(opposite page)
Composite trailers operated in trains of steel motor cars for more than a decade.[AL/EBW]

An eight car express train rolls over Manhattan valley
with a derby topped motorman at the controls. The
pin stripping is still visible but not for long. *(JG)*

Its the first use of the new steel cars and they look it. The use of
semaphore signals on the El mirror the mainline steam roads of the time.

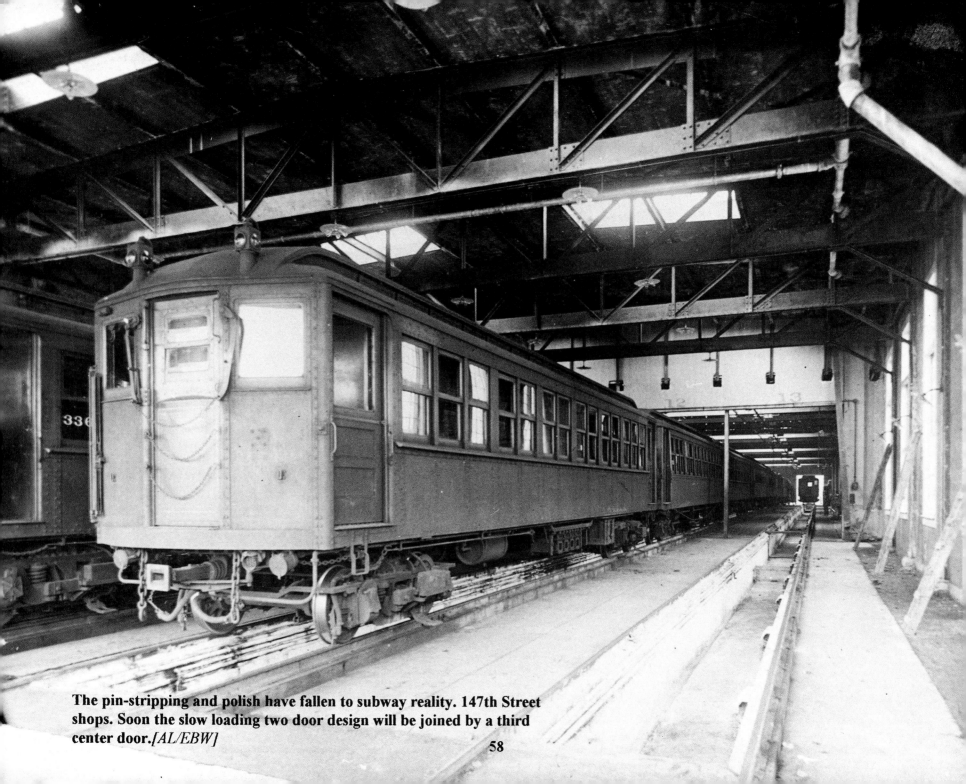

The pin-stripping and polish have fallen to subway reality. 147th Street shops. Soon the slow loading two door design will be joined by a third center door.*[AL/EBW]*

58

NOTICE
ALL PERSONS ARE FORBIDDEN TO
ENTER UPON OR CROSS THE TRACKS

The once splendid first steel subway cars enter the once splendid City Hall
station many years after the new subway was a thrill to see and ride.
[NG]
59

A temporary inspection barn was built at the north end of 180th Street station. A mix of steel and composite cars being worked on. In the distance a New York Westchester & Boston, Stillwell designed MU is operating. *[AL/EBW]*

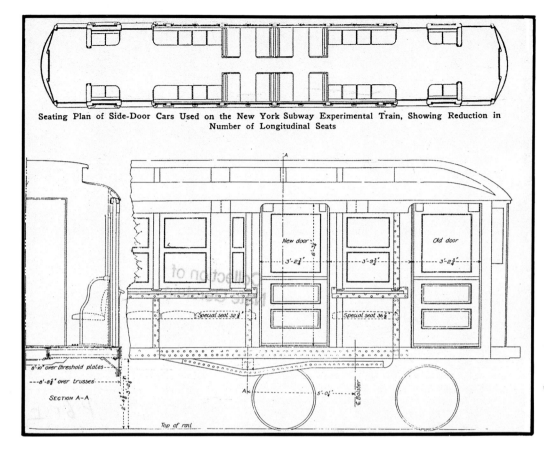

Seating Plan of Side-Door Cars Used on the New York Subway Experimental Train, Showing Reduction in Number of Longitudinal Seats

Several photos of the Bion J. Arnold door mechanism design. See pages *16-17* for details.
[AL/EBW]

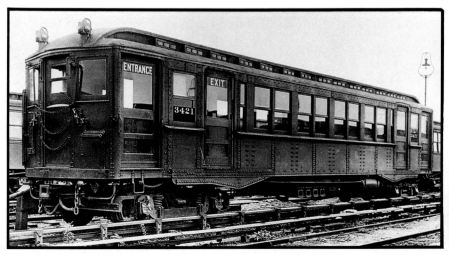

(Left) A proud motormen leans against his steed in this 1910 scene while a train whizzes by on the local track. *[NG]*
(Lower right)
3508 at Westchester yard. The Van Dorn link & pin couplers have been replaced with tight lock couplers.*[AL/EBW]*

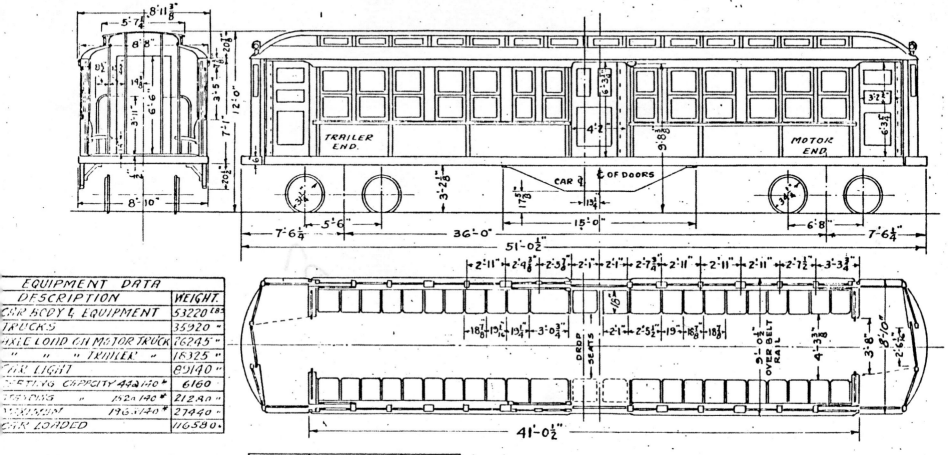

EQUIPMENT DATA	
DESCRIPTION	WEIGHT.
CAR BODY & EQUIPMENT	53220 LBS
TRUCKS	35920 "
AXLE LOAD ON MOTOR TRUCK	26245 "
" " " TRAILER "	18325 "
CAR LIGHT	89140 "
SEATING CAPACITY 44 @ 140 #	6160
STANDING " 152 @ 140 #	21280
MAXIMUM 196 @ 140 #	27440 "
CAR LOADED	116580 "

TRAILER END.

MOTOR END.

CAR ♀ OF DOORS

BUILDER	SERIAL Nºs	DATE.
A.C.&F.Co.	3517	JUNE, 04 APR. 05
"	3519 TO 3523	" "
"	3525 " 3566	" "
"	3568 " 3590	" "
"	3592 " 3600	" "
"	3602 " 3617	" "
"	3619 " 3624	" "
"	3626 " 3635	" "
"	3637	" "
"	3639 TO 3643	" "
"	3645 " 3649	" "

ONE CAR (3352) SOLD TO SEASHORE ELEC. RY (MUSEUM)
ALL OTHER CARS IN THIS SERIES SCRAPPED.

TOTAL - 123 MOTOR CARS.

SUPERSEDES DWG Nº 6637 E.

OUTLINE DRAWING.
1904-SUBWAY CAR (M.U.D.C.)
INTERBOROUGH RAPID TRANSIT CO.
CAR EQUIPMENT DEPT.
NEW YORK CITY. SHEET Nº 14635

3586 at Elder Ave. Pelham line in 1934.*[GV]*
p66-67

(Opposite page)
**Interior of Gibbs car after modifications with
fans, porcelain hand holds and center doors.**
[AL/EBW]

125 Street with a Gibbs motor leading.

3478 freshly painted on the 7th Ave.
Local at 125 Street.*[AL/EBW]*

3563 in a more tranquil scene at 125 St.
It has been converted recently to multiple
unit door control-note new doors and canvas
covered reversing mechanism on the door
edges. Do you remember
Rheingold beer?

3507 all alone at the back of 148th St. shops. While smaller in size an IRT subway car had a more rugged appearance when compared to a BMT Standard or an IND R-1 to R-9 standard car. *[AL/EBW]*

3432 in 1939 has thirty five years of service and still looks like she
is ready for another thirty five or more years of service. *[AL/EBW]*

Gibbs car at Chamber Street on the 7th Avenue line. Soon it will be under the East river headed for Brooklyn. *[EC]*

(Top)
OOPS! Through steel is durable it can be
terribly unforgiving of carelessness! Gibbs
motors Pelham line 1922. *(Bottom)* 3591
148 St.yards 1952.

(Left)
Gibbs awaiting rush hour service center track of the Pelham. *[EC]*

3638 & 3483 with the original steel car 3342 between them while in work service. NYW&B former station at 180th St. *[AL/EBW]*

72

Gibbs in work service had headlights add on their roofs like the composite cars in El service. *[EC]*

Gibbs motor at Van Cortlandt Park near the end of its career.

(Left) 3350-the"Original" spent most of its life after 1920 as Queens pay car in Corona yards.*(Bottom)* Having run their last mile Gibbs cars await the end.

(Left) **3352 on the way to its new home at the Seashore Trolley Museum Kennebunk Port Maine.**
(Bottom) **The End! The scrapper's torch awaits these cars on the grounds of the old "Star Lite" amusement park.**
[all AL/EBW]

DECK ROOF CARS

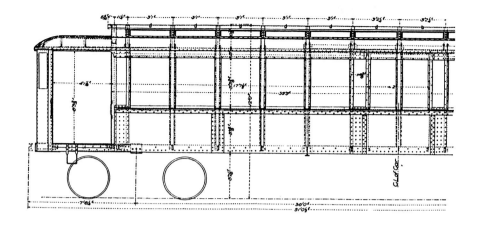

3661 at ACF Plant 1908. *[GV]*

(Right)
Deck roof cars on the Dyre Ave. Shuttle.
(Top)
Deck roof cars on the former NYW&B
station at East 180 St.-used as a terminal
for the Dyre Ave. Shuttle from 1941-1957.
[EC]

Deck roof motors were being displaced by
new R17 stock when this train awaited rush
hour service at Castle Hill Ave on Feb.26, 1956.
[NG]

3683 in summer, in the Bronx with the rear door open. *[AL/EBW]*

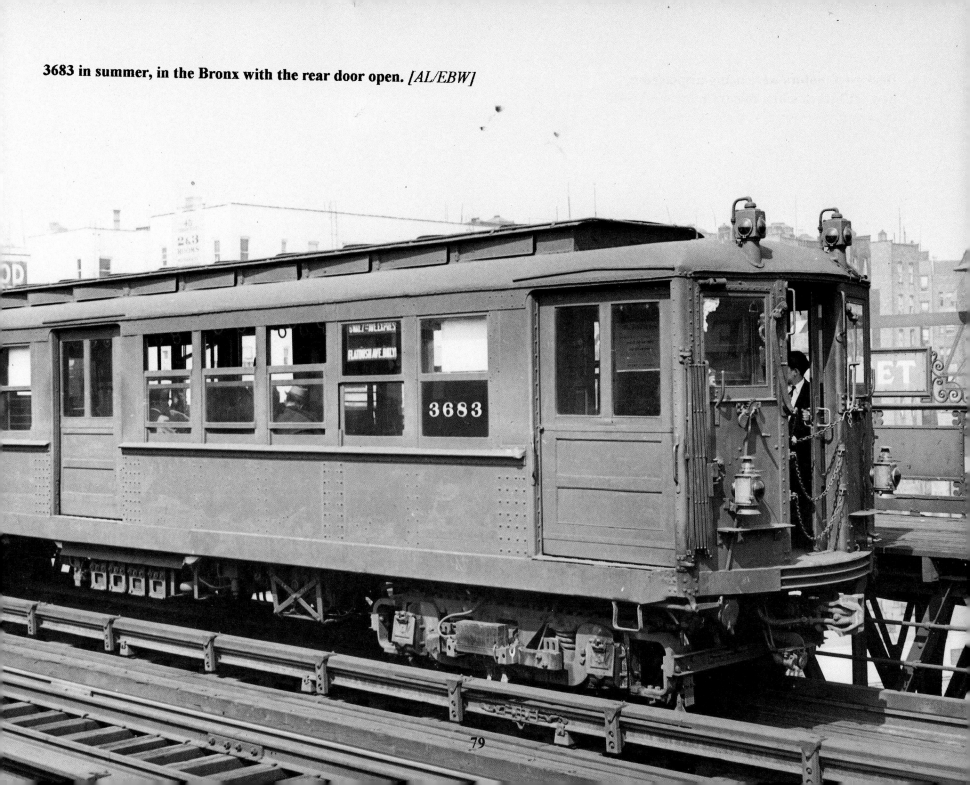

(Bottom)
3698 at 239 St. yard in 1954.
(Left)
3684-85 stored 239 St. yard in 1957.

(Left)
3680 the rear of a Broadway express 1936.
[GV]
(bottom)
3698 two decades previous at the Sound view Ave.
Station of the Pelham line. [AL/EBW]

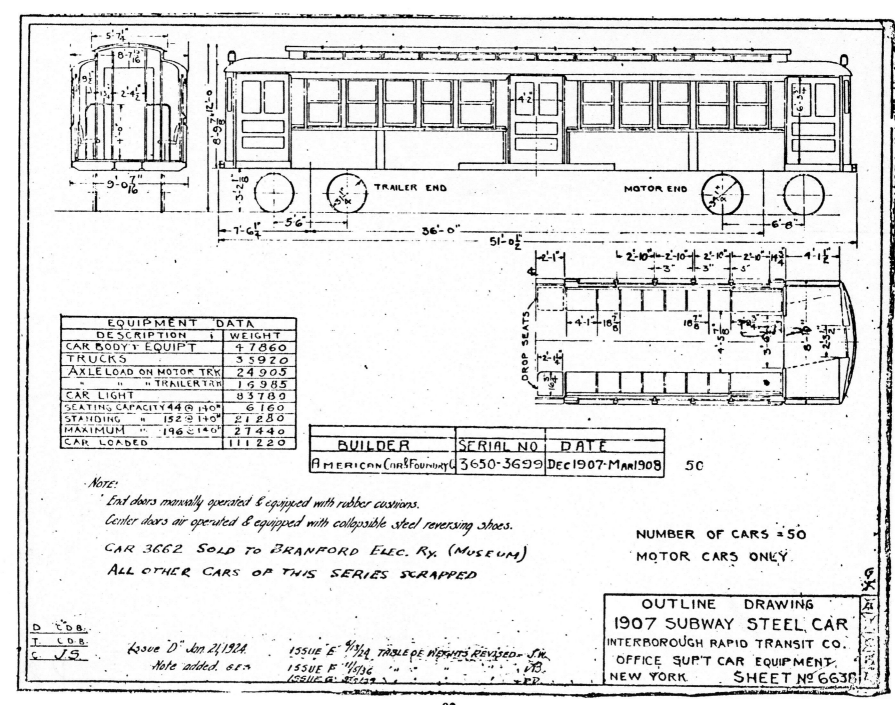

TRAILER END

MOTOR END

EQUIPMENT DATA	
DESCRIPTION	WEIGHT
CAR BODY & EQUIP'T	47860
TRUCKS	35920
AXLE LOAD ON MOTOR TRK	24905
" " " TRAILER TRK	16985
CAR LIGHT	83780
SEATING CAPACITY 44 @ 140#	6160
STANDING " 152 @ 140#	21280
MAXIMUM " 196 @ 140#	27440
CAR LOADED	111220

DROP SEATS

BUILDER	SERIAL NO	DATE
American Car & Foundry Co	3650-3699	Dec 1907 - Mar 1908

50

NOTE:
End doors manually operated & equipped with rubber cushions.
Center doors air operated & equipped with collapsible steel reversing shoes.

CAR 3662 SOLD TO BRANFORD ELEC. RY. (MUSEUM)
ALL OTHER CARS OF THIS SERIES SCRAPPED

NUMBER OF CARS = 50
MOTOR CARS ONLY

D C.D.B.
T. C.D.B.
C. J.S.

Issue "D" Jan 21, 1924.
Note added. G.E.F.

ISSUE E 4/8/24 TABLE OF WEIGHTS REVISED - S.W.
ISSUE F 11/5/36 " " " J.B.
ISSUE G 9/5/42 " " " P.P.

OUTLINE DRAWING
1907 SUBWAY STEEL CAR
INTERBOROUGH RAPID TRANSIT CO.
OFFICE SUP'T CAR EQUIPMENT
NEW YORK.   SHEET No 6630

Center foreground Deck roofers
on Dyre Ave. Shuttle 1954.
(bottom)
Deck roofers working the 42nd St. shuttle.

PLATFORM MAN
012355
INTERBOROUGH RAPID TRANSIT CO.

3662 Starred in the Fifth Avenue Associations Golden Anniversary parade with brand new R22 #7526 on Oct. 10, 1957.

3662 rolls out of the 147 Street shop for the parade.*[AL/EBW]*

(Top)
3662 with R-type cars and standard car at E.180 St.
(Middle)
A happier fate awaited 3662-preservation at the Shore line Trolley Museum at East Haven, Connecticut.
(Bottom)
Gutted by the scrappers torch July 1, 1957.

HEDLEY HiV CARS

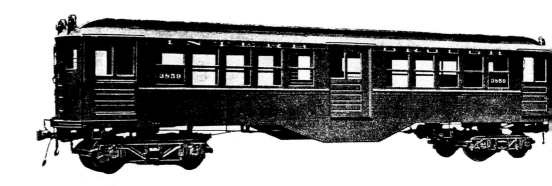

Hedley motor 3995 at Third Ave.
El shop at 99 Street.

Brand new Hedley motor at 147 St. Shop 1911. *[AL/EBW]*

3940

3983 Hedley motor at 181 St. 1956

Hedley HiV on rear of Broadway local near 120 St. 1956. *[NG]*

(Top)
4022 at the end of the line at Grand Central terminal, on what was once the uptown express track when it was part of the first main line. *[AL/EBW]*

(Right)
3967 looks neat even while it is grimy because it is in service which gives it life even with the subway grim.*[CEO]*

(Left)
One of the only two Hedley HiV motor cars not equipped with multiple unit door control-125th Street station 1940.
(Bottom)
3998 heads the introductory ten car train-January 1911.
[AL/EBW]

Standard HiV in their waning years-July 1956. *[NG]*.

Standard HiV departing 168th Street-1956. *[NG]*

P 18543. L 4326. 7-30-15. P.V.V.

Fliver 4037 arriving from Pullman 1915. *[AL/EBW]*

FLIVERS

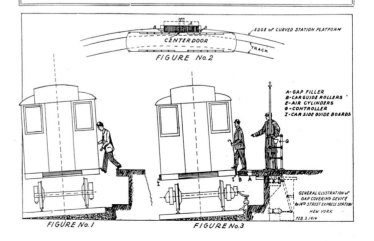

roadway local with rear Flivver car partly in the sun light.

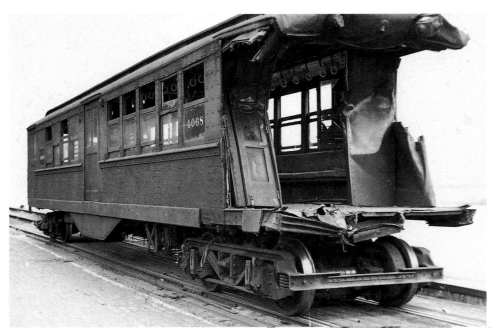

Interborough Bulletin

OCTOBER, 1914   Vol. IV, No. 10

SAFETY

SAFETY FIRST

OUR PERPETUAL PROMPTER

(OPPOSITE PAGE)
Flivver 4111 slows down for flagman near Jackson and Prospect Avenues.
(TOP)
Not an open observation car but 4068 got itself into a little scrap with LoV car 5297. See page 119

IRT trailers even look like they are all business even when alone resting. 4198 in 1939 at 180th St. yard.
[AL/EBW]

149th Street station with new florescent lighting added. *[EC]*

4096 in work service on the Pelham line. *[AL/EBW]*

4158 at 174th St.
[AL/EBW]

4211 being scrapped on March 28,1964.
[AL/EBW]

LoV CARS

From the Berwick plant of AC&F 5618 is ready for delivery sans all electrical and interior work.

From the Berwick plant of AC&F 5618 is ready for delivery sans all electrical and interior work.

(TOP)
**The cockpit of a standard IRT car with controler
 handle on the left, brake stand minus brake handle
 on right with the whistle valve and the black box
 on the window which indicated that all automatic
 doors were closed.**
(LEFT)
5618 without electrical equipment

(Top)
Interior of Low Voltage car prior
installation of seats.
(Bottom)
Long view of the same car.

102

(Right)
4625 among other equipment in
148th St. yard in 1919.
(Bottom)
Later Low Voltage cars at left.
High Voltage Gibbs & Deck
Roofers at right-1919.
[AL/EBW]

Low Voltage, Steinway, Instruction car and Mineola congregate at 148th St. yard in 1919.
[AL/EBW]

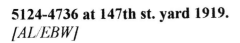

5124-4736 at 147th st. yard 1919.
[AL/EBW]

(Left)
5135 on Broadway express 207th St. station in 1946.
(Bottom)
4600 on Broadway at 125th St. In 1924.

4568 heads a train of Low Voltage cars on the Pelham line. *[NG]*

(TOP RIGHT)
Looking out the front door made dreamers of us all.
(BOTTOM)
South bound 4588 with seven cars coming into Buhre Ave. Station.*[EC]*

Low Voltage 5160 in Mosholu yard. *[AL/EBW]*

Interior of Low Voltage car awaiting service on White Plains Road. *[AL/EBW]*

Low Voltage motors Mosholu yard 1933.*[AL/EBW]*

5435 in 180th yard in 1926. *[AL/EBW]*

This late scene north of 180th Street station should be compared with the same scene on page 60. Some of the NYW & B shop structures are still around today.

LoVs have new R-type
head lights but semaphores are still
in use on the once IRT line.

Some Bronx residents had a great railfan parlor window to observe the operations of the IRT.

114

5214 stands at ease in 240th St. yard. *[AL/EBW]*

Car 5160 interior typical of the Interborough. *[AL/EBW]*

Low Voltage cars in work service entering Fordham Road Jerome Avenue about 1964 [HS]

(Left)
This was a common sight, a hot day an the motorman could open his door a crack. This on the Dyre Avenue line in 1955. *[AL/EBW]*

(Bottom)
5341 a waiting rush hour service in the year 1937. *[AL/EBW]*

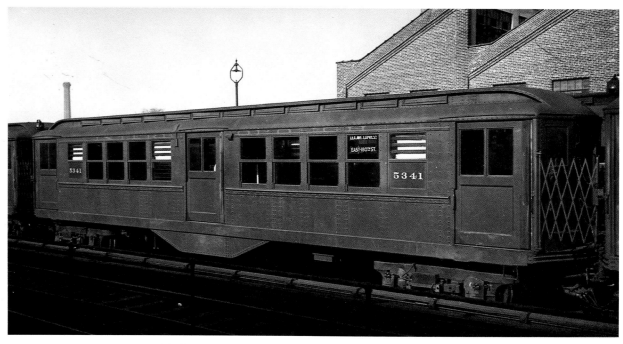

(Right)
147th st. Yard crunch! Amid the 1953 fleet.
(Bottom)

Because most of the IRT lines were four
track lines, LoV cars running in fast
express service were right at home and
they could move. *[SZ]*

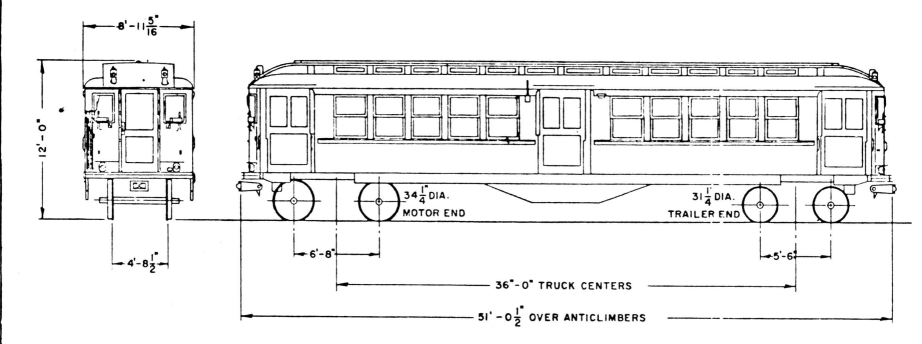

8'-11 5/16"

12'-0"

4'-8 1/2"

34 1/4" DIA.
MOTOR END

31 1/4" DIA.
TRAILER END

6'-8"

5'-6"

36"-0" TRUCK CENTERS

51'-0 1/2" OVER ANTICLIMBERS

TOTAL WEIGHT 77,050 LBS

GENERAL DATA

EQUIPMENT		TRUCKS			MISCELLANEOUS	
CONTROL TYPE	G.E. PC-10 W.H 214-B	NUMBER & TYPE	HEDLEY-BAR		DATE BUILT	1917
CONTROLLER & MASTER CONTROL	C-1-131-B	WEIGHT OF MOTOR TRUCK	20,848	25,400	SEATING CAPACITY	
TYPE OF BRAKING	AMUE-ME23	WGT. OF TRAILER TRUCK	10,146	11,100	FANS	4-PADDLE
COMPRESSOR	D3F	MOTORS	GE 260			
BRAKE CYLINDER	18 x 12	TRIP COCK	FISH TAIL			
HAND BRAKE						
COUPLERS	F-H2-MCB					
DRAFT GEAR	WAUGH					
DOOR ENGINES	——					
CONDUIT	——					
BATTERIES	B4H					

NEW YORK CITY TRANSIT AUTHORITY
CAR MAINT DEPT.

402-2001
SHEET 195

Some Low Voltage cars were modified with platform spacer for BMT service in 1959.

4586-4587 on Culver line
Dec.4, 1959.

4588 also on Culver line
Aug. 1,1959.

4601 modified for BMT
service also 1959. *[AL/EBW]*

Steinways roll out of Queens Plaza bound for Astoria, 1945. *[NG]*

STEINWAYS

(Top)
Steinway #4763 arrives from the Pullman Company on A Michigan Central RR flat car-1916. [AL/EBW]
(left)
Steinway #4722 departs Hunters Point Ave. in July 1948, the same month that the R12 cars will begin displacing the "Interborough Fleet" from Queens. [AL/EBW]

4702 in Corona yard 1949. [*AL/EBW*]

(Left)
4700 Freshly painted for the
World's Fair 1938. *[AL/EBW]*
(Bottom)
4575 on the Flushing line 1936.
[AL/EBW]

4756 leads train of Steinways at the 174 St-West Farms Elevated. *[EC]*

(Left)
Steinways climb out of the tunnel at Hunters Point Ave in 1948. *[AL/EBW]*
(Bottom)
4763, 4704 on the Polo Grounds shuttle at 167 St and Jerome. *[AL/EBW]*

(Left)
Original Steinway 4029.
(Bottom)
5630 & 5637 at 149 St. & Third Ave. in 1964.

4738 Steinway at 169 St. in service on the Third Ave. El in the Bronx. BMT Q-type cars are laid up on the express track.*[AL/EBW]*
(Bottom)
Steinways departing Gun Hill Road on the Third Ave. El -Feb. 22, 1957.*[AL/EBW]*

WORLDS FAIR CARS

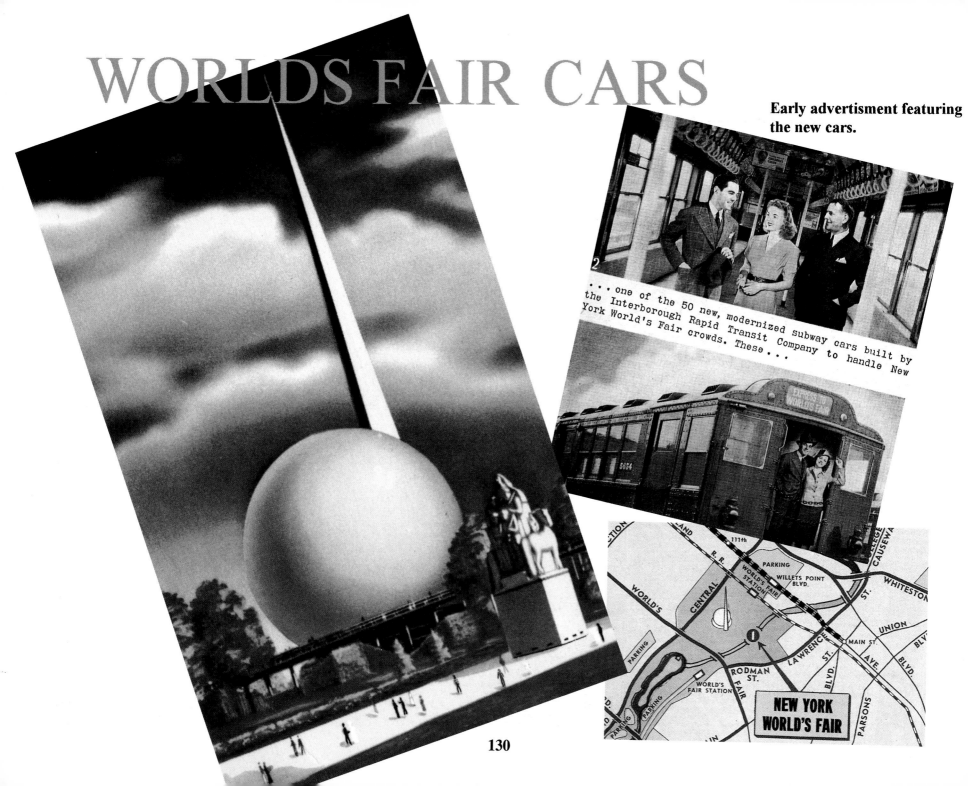

Early advertisment featuring the new cars.

. . . one of the 50 new, modernized subway cars built by the Interborough Rapid Transit Company to handle New York World's Fair crowds. These . . .

NEW YORK WORLD'S FAIR

(Top right)
Framing of World's Fair car.
(Bottom left)
The car takes on a shape.
(Bottom right)
The completed shells.

(Top left)
Completed cars await painting.
(Top right)
Ready for shipment to New York
(Lower left)
Rolling off to the big city and the fair.

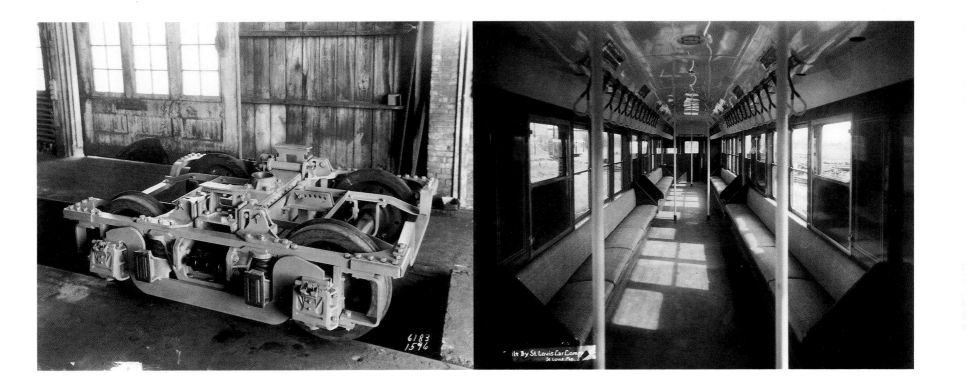

(Top right)
Trucks for the World Fair cars.
(Top)
Interior of the World's Fair car.
(Lower right)
5656 departing New Haven's Harlem River freight yard for the Interborough property(the Third Ave. El).

133

The fleet assembled in Corona yard.
The Flushing line, Willets Pt.
Blvd. Tower and new sub-
station stand on the horizon.

With operating components
installed, the new World's
Fair cars pose for their
portrait at the 147 St. Shop.

(Top)
5654 at the rear of a train returning from the fair.

5685 sports World's Fair insignia.
[AL/EBW]

137

(Top)
**5689 in Flushing local service
at 74th St. 1939**
(Lower right)
Arriving at Willets Pt. Blvd.

(Top)
5659 in World's Fair service during the first year of the fair. *[GV]*

(Lower right)
5659 leads a Manhattan bound local into the Rawson St. station. The huge Breyer's ice cream sign a Queens landmark for decades *[AL/EBW]*

(Lower right)
On their last assignment, World's Fair motors plied the last remnat of the Third Avenue El in the Bronx from 1962-1969. They were the most modern cars to run on the El.

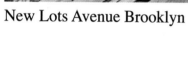

New Lots Avenue Brooklyn

In Third Avenue service, a WF motor under the charge of a uniformed motorman(complete with neck tie)arrives at Fordham Road. *[HS]*

INTERBOROUGH FLEET

(as built-1903-1940)

Experimental Composite Cars:
3340 Originally experimental # 1 "August Belmont."
3341 Originally experimental # 2 "John B. McDonald."

Unpowered (trailer) Composite Cars:
2000-2059	Jewett Car Co.	1903-04
2060-2119	St. Louis Car Co.	"
2120-2159	Wason Car Co.	"

Composite Motor Cars:
3000-3039	Jewett Co.	1903-04
3040-3139	Stephenson Car Co.	"
3140-3279	St. Louis Car Co.	"
3280-3339	Wason Car Co.	"

Experimental Steel Car:
3342 Pennsylvania Railroad-Altoona Shop 1903

"Gibbs" Steel Motor Cars:
3350-3549	Amer. Car & Fndry	1904-05*
3550-3649	"	1905

"Deck Roof" Steel Motor Cars:
3650-3699	Amer, Car & Fndry	1907-08

Standard ("Hedley") all-steel fleet:
Standard Motor cars constructed with "High Voltage" controls:
3700-3809	Amer. Car & Fndry	1910-11
3810-3849	Standard Steel Car Co.	1910-11
3850-4024	Pressed Steel Car Co.	1910-11

Standard Motor and Trailer cars built by the Pullman Company in 1915-16 incorporating operating components salvaged from Composite fleet:

4037-4160	"Flivver" Motor Cars
4161-4222	"Flivver" Trailer Cars*
4223-4514*	Trailer cars for **"High Voltage"** cars **3350-4024**

Standard motor cars with *"Low Voltage"* controls:

4577-4699	Pullman Co.	1916-17*
4771-4810	"	"
4966-5301	"	1917
5403-5502	Amer. Car & Fndry	1924
5503-5627	"	"

Standard trailer cars with *"Low Voltage"* controls:

4515-4576	Pullman Co.	1916-17*
4811-4825	"	"
4826-4965	"	1917
5302	" (non revenue car)	"
5303-5377	"	1922
5378-5402	"	1922

Standard *"Steinway"* Motor Cars for Queensborough service through Steinway tunnel:

4025-4036	Pressed Steel Car Co.	1915
4700-4771	"	1916-17
5628-5652	Amer. Car & Fndry	1926

"World's Fair" cars with redesigned body:

5653-5702	St. Louis Car Co.	1938

*Note:*Original Gibbs Car **#3350** assigned to non-revenue service on Queensborough lines from early 1920s to retirement in 1950s. Trailer cars **#4215-4222** and **4555-4576** were converted to Steinway motor cars at the 129th Street shops of the Manhattan Company in 1929. Likewise, trailers **#4223-4242** were converted to "blind" (no operating cab) motor cars with High Voltage controls in 1952. **#4243-4250** followed in 1955. Low Voltage motor cars **4581, 4583, 4585-4605** were fitted with side spacer flanges for operation on BMT Franklin and Culver shuttles from 1959-1961.

5302 was a LoV with out a center door. Here seen at E180 Street yard in April 1952. The car was used to collect the millions of nickels on the system for many years. *[AL/EBW]*

HISTORICAL NOTES

It appears that selection of the manual acceleration control system in 1903 was the result of an effort to repeat the phenomenal operating success of the Manhattan Railway electrification program. The Interborough cars employed a propulsion system which was a more powerful refinement of the 1899-1900 design installed on the Manhattan cars. By the time the subway opened in 1904, automatic acceleration was available but the company was unwilling to experiment with radical technology. That conservatism persisted until 1915, by which time automatic acceleration was well proven on the cars of both the Long Island Rail Road and the Brooklyn Rapid Transit elevated network.

The electric Christenson air pumps installed on the Composite and Gibbs steel cars were replaced after a few years by Westinghouse Air Brake Co. units of the standard "D" series. Furthermore, the conversion to Westinghouse "tightlock" couplers in place of the original Van Dorn link and pin couplers was the result of frequent instances in which trains uncoupled while in public service. The tightlock design was adopted in 1909 in view of the planned operation of ten car trains.

There is some confusion in regard to the use of the term "battleships" by the train crews. While it was thought to refer to the steel motor cars constructed in 1910-11 (# 3700-4024) possibly as a result of all the attention accorded the visit of the U.S. Navy fleet to the city at that time, other sources attribute the term to a statement made by George Gibbs to the effect that his pioneer steel car design would be as sturdy as a battleship.

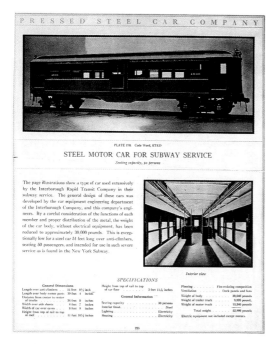

A Pressed Steel Ad that shows a Pullman product. *[JG]*

The once prestigious car number one the August Belmont delivered on August 2 1902 would in a very short time spend most of her years as car 3340 but if it could no longer inspire people with its beauty it inspired their minds and was used to train thousands of IRT motormen and maintainers. *[AL/EBW]*

MINNIE WAS A LADY

by E.J.Quinby

Without taint of scandal, it may now be told. The railroad tycoon August P. Belmont had a sweetheart and her name was Minnie.

A born aristocrat, she was raised in luxury. People admired her scarlet costume and bright gold trim. They regarded with pleasure her Empire adornments, her silver service, and her plush comforts. They agreed that the colorful leaded glass enhanced her beauty.

The proud August kept his lady in proper style, sparing no expense to show her off. A white-coated waiter, in answer to push-button calls, served Minnie's guests with rare imported wines and caviar and the like.

Maybe you've guest it by now. Minnie was the private and palatial subway car, and her real name was Mineola.

Belmont also built the New York City Interborough, a trolley line that started in Manhattan at 155th Street, crossed the Harlem River to traverse the Bronx, and recrossed the Harlem River to 181st Street, Manhattan. The ride cost only a nickel, with three cent transfer, if desired, to the Elevated at 155th Street or to the subway at 181st Street. The first four-motor trolleys to appear in New York were built to negotiate the steep Ogden Avenue hill on this line.

It was Belmont who built the tunnels under the East River at 42nd Street to bring the Long Island trolleys right into Grand Central. Having completed these tubes and equipped them with overhead trolley wire, he acquired a fleet a fleet of all steel , multiple-unit trolleys for the through service between Grand Central and Flushing. Political obstacles prevented continuation of this service after the opening demonstration runs, and the tubes, idle for years, filled up with river water. But eventually the service was established, and Belmont's Interborough subway trains began using these tunnels for the run to Flushing.

Belmont was famous in his day. He acquired control of New York's Manhattan Elevated Railway and retired its puffing little Forney locomotives in favor of complete electrification in 1903. It was Belmont who, after years of unsuccessful efforts to do so with municipal funds, financed the original subway system for the city-and combined the Manhattan Elevated lines to form one, integrated, city-wide transit system.

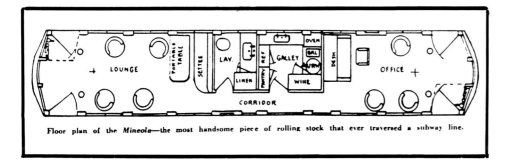

Floor plan of the *Mineola*—the most handsome piece of rolling stock that ever traversed a subway line.

It was August P. Belmont who built the Pelham Bay Monorail line, from Bartow station on the New Haven to City Island. Although decades ahead of its time, it foreshadowed the modern systems now being designed for big metropoli. Belmont was daring and progressive, a man of action who had the financial resources to carry out his visionary plans. When he got behind a project, bankers were ready and willing to put up the necessary money.

In those days, Grand Central area was a real vortex of teeming New York City. As the Interborough Subway construction progressed up Fourth Avenue, it became necessary to curve the line westward across 42nd Street to reach Broadway at Times Square, whence the line was to continue up Broadway. But the big heavy subway trains could not negotiate a sharp street corner as trolleys could, and it was clear that the line would have to "cut across lots" in making the bend. The alert August, who was way ahead of the planning engineers, had already

acquired the strategic property on the southwest corner of 42nd Street at Fourth (now Park) Avenue. So he sold the desired curved underground to the Interborough Corporation, reserving rights to build what he wanted above ground at that point. What he wanted to build, and what he did build, was the Belmont Hotel. In its basement was a "circular" bar, designed to fit inside the radius of the subway curve. It quickly became a popular rendezvous. The Belmont has vanished now, but the line across 42nd Street still remains as the shuttle.

August Belmont was a bon vivant of the first order. One of his hobbies was race horses, and he acquired quite a stable of fine-bred steeds. It was he who established Belmont Park out on Long Island near, Mineola, with its splendid track, commodious stables, and big grandstand. There he also built a sumptuous club-house, and when the Long Island was electrifying its commuter lines, he arranged with them to extend a spur right into his Belmont Park for the benefit of race fans.

One day Belmont called in his engineers of the Interborough subway project, and sprang a surprise on them that captured their imagination. August wanted a private subway car. Presidents of other railroads enjoyed the facilities of a private car, why not Belmont too? Wasn't he entitled to the same consideration? It was quickly agreed that this was quite in order, and with the cooperation of the Wason Car Company of Springfield Massachusetts, plans and specifications were quickly drawn up. The result was the most handsome item of rolling stock that ever traversed a subway line.

The Mineola emerged as a beautiful vehicle, with the interior trim of natural mahogany, artistically inlaid. Curved plate glass windows to fit the bumper contour, extended from the roof to the floor at each end, providing an unobstructed view of the line ahead and behind. There was an oval stained glass window in each side. Between two large compartments at each end, the interior contained a corridor which bypassed the steward's galley and the levorotatory, both completely equipped with hot and cold running water. The galley contained electric grille and an electric oven, as well as a refrigerator, a pantry and well stocked wine locker. A nickel plated electric coffee urn with faucet was installed to provide hot coffee on tap at all times.

One of the large end compartments contained an upholstered settee, placed against the bulkhead, while the other end compartment contained Belmont's private roll-top desk, also against the bulkhead. The arched Empire ceiling was tinted a pistachio green, with gold trim. To fit this contour above the bulkheads, decorative stain glass panels were installed. A set of folding glass doors at each end could be adjusted to form a booth for the motorman, off to the right, where he and the controls could be enclosed without obstructing the view ahead. Individual chairs stood on a broadloom carpet. Portable tables could be set up by the steward upon request.

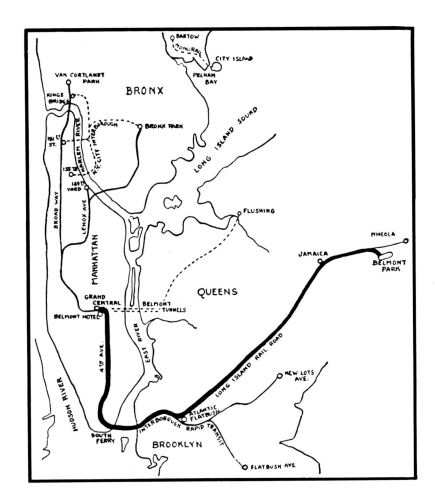

In addition to the decorative lighting fixtures, there were polished brass gages and meters arranged where Belmont could observe the speed, the air pressure, the voltage, and the current. Mineola's exterior was a distinctive as her interior. She was finished in glossy maroon, with gold leaf striping and lettering. Along the letterboards, she bore the inscription INTERBOROUGH, while along her sides beneath the belt-rail, she bore the name **MINEOLA**, also in gold.

The sad look of a neglected Mineola when it arrived at Brandford Trolley Museum. *[AL/EBW]*

The interior of Mineola at the Gioscia farm. *[NYCTA]*

The Interborough subway construction crossed the East River near South Ferry to reach Brooklyn, and the line was extended out to the Flatbush-Atlantic Avenue terminal to the newly electrified Long Island Rail Road. Here Belmont made a deal with the Long Island to put in a connecting switch. There was a reason. The same reason prompted installation of a private door leading into the Interborough Subway from the basement of the Belmont Hotel. Minnie had an important role to perform.

When the proud August had made all the necessary preparations, he organized the first trip to the Belmont Park establishment via electric railway right from his Belmont Hotel. His select party of guests met in his private chambers up in the hotel, and when all was ready, Belmont led them straight down to the basement. Maybe they paused at the circular bar, but this would not have been really necessary, for Minnie's steward was expecting them. Through the secret passage, Belmont led his surprised guests, right into the luxurious private car.

When they all were comfortably seated and all the doors were shut, August waved a signal and they were off to the races! The steward served champagne as they raced down along the express track. As they plunged beneath the East River, the steward passed the caviar. When Mineola reached the Long Island terminal at Flatbush-Atlantic Avenue, the towerman had the switches all lined up for her, and the Belmont party rolled right through the Long Island terminal, and out over the line through Brooklyn.

Soon they were racing along lush fields and green trees. They eased through the busy junction at Jamaica, and when the palatial private car reached the race track spur, it was switched right into the grounds, and came to rest at the Clubhouse where the affable Major Domo awaited them. Minnie's first trip to the race track was a great success. Re-iced and re-provisioned, she stood until the meet was over that day, and brought the party swiftly back to the Belmont Hotel at Grand Central.

Thereafter, Minnie popularity increased and her fame spread amongst the elite. Mayor Mc Cellan was often her guest. So were Lillian Russell, Diamond Jim Brady, Theodore P. Shonts, Frank Hedley, Frank Shepard, Frank Sprague, the Astors and the Vanderbilts.

Belmont took Minnie on inspection trips over his Interborough system. She served on many important occasions as the scene of important private conferences in which sizable business deals were consummated. But when Belmont passed to his rewards, Minnie was shunted into the backshop, where she reposed while the transit scene underwent radical changes. When space came to premium, Minnie was given a tight shroud of canvas tarpaulins, and shifted to the corner of the yard, out in the weather up at 149th Street & Lenox Avenue

Starving on the five cent fare which the city refused to increase, the Interborough proprietors finally threw in the sponge, and the City of New York took over the property, straightway raising the fare to ten cents, then to fifteen. Most of the old timers on the line had either retired, died, or moved to greener pastures, and Minnie become the forgotten car. Then one day some representatives of the city administration became inquisitive about the curious enshrouded object over in one corner of the 149th Street yard.
"Wonder what's under those covers, Mack?"

"Maybe just another wreck that was never repaired, and they wanted to conceal the bad publicity from view." suggested the other. " Let's rip off the covers and see what we've inherited here." And that was how Minnie came to light in recent years. "We can't use that thing in revenue service. What good is it?" "No use to us. Let's scrap it or sell it to a junkie."

So it came to pass that one Schiovoni, dealer in scrap, acquired the magnificent Mineola. He had the good sense not to put her to the torch, however. He removed the trucks, couplers, and under-body gear, and sent Minnie out to a friend who owned a farm in New Jersey, "Pappa Gioscia can use that thing for a chicken coop, or something," he mused.

But when Minnie arrived at the farmstead on a low-bed truck, Pappa Gioscia took one admiring look at her, and decided that she should be his own private retreat, where he could get away from his noisy grandchildren, to smoke and read.

So Minnie was mounted on a concrete foundations under her body bolsters, and Pappa Gioscia enjoyed privacy in her artistocratic appointments for several years. Now he, too, has passed to his rewards. And Minnie waits, amid serene surroundings.

ADDENDUM

This is basically where the Railroad magazine1956 story ended. The car was transfered to a collection at Bloomsburg Pa. and suffered from flood. The Shoreline Trolley Museum (Brandford trolley Museum) of East Branford Connectecut acquired in 1972. At this writting (1997) proposals have been made to restore the car for the centennial of the IRT in 2004.

149

IRT IN COLOR

(Left) A new IRT train under the East River in this early tinted post-card. *[NG]*

◄

Restored LoV cars 5443, 5483, 5466, 5290 & 5292 on an ERA excursion. *[DG]*

A post-card depicting the yet to be opened subway. Note the vault lighting over the platform . *[JCG]* ▼

5443 on display at Chambers Street on the BMT, 3-23-79. *[EC]*

Museum LoV's at Willets Point with Shea Stadium in the distance. *[EO]*

Side view of the colorful 5443. *[EC]*

5290 at 149th St. & 3rd Avenue on an
ERA fan trip.

5292 at Burnside Avenue, Jerome Line
in 1979.

LoV's pass the house that Ruth built.

◄ 239th street yard is a sea of various IRT equipment. *[EC]*

▼ Jerome yard before modern cars and construction of an apartment complex that would cover the yard.*[CEO]*

◄

(Opposite page) **April 29 1973 and it's farewell to the El. This is the last train on the 3rd Avenue El. The train is at Claremont Parkway. *[DG]***

A deck roof car takes up the rear of a Polo. *[CEO]*

A warm fall evening and Steinway in 1962.

▼ The snow has finally stopped, but the 3rd Avenue moves on.

▼ World's Fair, Steinways and LoV car in a train at 210th St.-Williamsbridge in the Bronx. *[DG]*

For decades this was the image of the Bronx with black IRT cars curving round El structures and surface Macks ran the streets. *[CEO]*

▼ The Giants have left New York and soon the Polo Grounds will disappear behind a LoV that crosses the Harlem River. *[CEO]*

5302 was an IRT oddity for it was built without a center door. *[DG]*

▼ Interior of a LoV in its final years of service. *[CEO]*

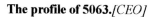 A clean museum train passes the
IND Bedford Park yards.*[CEO]*

The profile of 5063.*[CEO]*

Restored LoV's in a shot that
would warm any IRT fans
heart. *[CEO]*

You can almost hear the motors. *[CEO]*

5230 is being looked over for any defects. *[EC]*

IRT cars had a big storm door window to view the mysteries of the IRT. *[CEO]*

So after decades of service the end has come for 4884. *[CEO]*

157

(Top) Serving the line they were made for. No Shea Stadium in the background, yet. *[CEO]* (Bottom) Interior of 5687 at Gun Hill Road.*[CEO]*

(Top) In the last stages of service WF cars took on sealed beam headlights and radio antenna under motorman window. (Bottom) WF still never looked modern. *[EC]*

(Top) 5654 being finished at Coney Island Paint shop.
(Bottom) A new life on the 3rd Avenue El at 204th St.*[EC]*

This is how good a WF car looks when maintained well.*[DG]*
(Bottom) An inglorious end as a WF works out its career
as a work horse.*[CEO]*

159

WORK SERVICE

Not a Turbo powered LoV but G236 Vacuum car ex 4954.
[Al/EBW]

Diesel class room car at Westchester yards.*[EC]*

A few LoV became snow plows on the Brighton Beach line. *[CEO]*

A strong looking work horse but still the passenger signs hang
in the window, as if it was hard to stop carrying passengers.*[CEO]*